Celebrating Young Children and Their Teachers

Also by Mimi Brodsky Chenfeld

Creative Experiences for Young Children

Teaching by Heart

Teaching in the Key of Life

The House at 12 Rose Street

Celebrating Young Children and Their Teachers

and Their Teachers

The
Mimi Brodsky Chenfeld
New and Selected Writings　　Reader

Mimi Brodsky Chenfeld

 Redleaf Press
www.redleafpress.org

 naeyc

Published by Redleaf Press
a division of Resources for Child Caring
10 Yorkton Court
St. Paul, MN 55117
Visit us online at www.redleafpress.org.

National Association for the Education of Young Children
1313 L Street NW, Suite 500
Washington, DC 20005
NAEYC order #7201

© 2007 by Mimi Brodsky Chenfeld

First edition 2007
Cover design by Lightbourne
Cover photograph by Allen Zak. Children in photograph are Trenton Hunter,
    Nora Butter, and Eli Helfgott
Interior typeset in Baskerville
Interior illustrations by Melissa Muldoon
Fabulous T-shirt design by Callie and Ryan Wilbat and friends
Printed in the United States of America
14 13 12 11 10 09 08 07   1 2 3 4 5 6 7 8

Redleaf Press books are available at a special discount when purchased in bulk for special premiums and sales promotions. For details, contact the sales manager at 800-423-8309.

Library of Congress Cataloging-in-Publication Data

Chenfeld, Mimi Brodsky.
  Celebrating young children and their teachers : the Mimi Brodsky Chenfeld reader : new and selected writings / Mimi Brodsky Chenfeld.
      p. cm.
  ISBN 978-1-933653-27-3
  1. Preschool teaching—United States—Anecdotes. 2. Early childhood education—United States—Anecdotes. 3. School children—Psychology—Anecdotes. I. Title.
  LB1140.23b .C435 2007
  372.21--dc22

                          2006029615

In memory of Iris and Joe Kaplan, Rose and Charles Chenfeld, and all our dear ones who went before us but are still with us every day

For my fantastic children: Cliff and Chana, Cara and Jim, Dan and Kristi

For my wonder-full grandchildren: Len, Callie, Dylan, Chloe, Ryan, Noah, and Landen

For YOU who love, care for, and teach ALL of our children

For Howard, always my center

Now, more than ever, we must walk together toward a world of love and peace

The following essays were published previously in *Teaching in the Key of Life* by the National Association for the Education of Young Children (NAEYC) in 1993:

I'm Worried about Our Children

"Wanna Play?"

"My Loose Is Tooth!" Kidding Around with the Kids

Can a Fish Snap Its Fingers?

We Drew a Circle That Took Him In

Words of Encouragement: Honey on the Page

These essays were published previously in *Teaching by Heart* by Redleaf Press in 2001:

"Do Spiderwebs Ever Wake You Up?" Why I Hang
     Out with the Kids

Let's Keep the "L" Word

Oh, No! Not the "L" Word Again

Snowball

The Whole Truth about Hole Language: Can You Dig It?

Get the Elephant Out of the Room: We're Finished
     with the "E"s

Telling Time

Schools Children Run To

A Letter to Families and Friends of the Children in
     Room 13

Celebrating Young Children and Their Teachers

Foreword

My mother, Margaret Pollitzer, an educator in the 1920s and '30s as wonderful as Mimi Chenfeld is today, used to say, "You can't be much of an educator if you're not much of a person." There it is in a nutshell. The best teachers include themselves in their classroom life.

I spend lots of time in schools and see a great many pleasant, competent technicians unfurling the printed curriculum for the *students*. Of course, to an extent we should and must do this. A rich curriculum is a good thing. Besides, we have to do what our supervisors expect us to do, which may be fantastic, although in some settings it's quite restrictive. Technician teachers leave it at that: they prepare and dole out the lessons and activities proficiently, stick to the schedule, keep their records up-to-date, and keep things clean and orderly—all these things, so many things, so many, many things—which goodness knows isn't easy to do! But terrific teachers add the spices of life to their offerings. Watching Mimi work with children of any age and with teachers (of any age), or reading her writings about it, reminds us of what these enlivening ingredients are.

She enjoys children. She enjoys people. She considers children people (not simply one-dimensional *students*). Interest in others, including each individual child, is an essential ingredient of educational excellence. Actually, the first two sentences in this paragraph are not factually correct: Mimi more than enjoys children and other people; she *delights* in them. Simply enjoying kids and being genuinely interested in their concerns, curiosities, fascinations, and feelings is, however, good enough.

Mimi also loves her *subject,* the integrated arts—music, singing, dancing, dramatics, creative writing, visual arts, all the arts, mixed and mingled as needed. Many teachers like one or more of these expressive activities, and if they dared, most could loosen up and participate in more of them with the children they teach. I join Mimi in shouting, "Dare to do it!" Reap the rewards of making children happy, of making friends with them by connecting in these physical and emotional ways, of fostering their love of learning and school. If you won't sing, can you play various kinds of interesting recorded music and schedule visiting musicians? If you don't dance, can you encourage children to enjoy moving to the music you play and find ways to let them see different kinds of dancers dancing? If your interests lie elsewhere—perhaps nature is your passion, or cooking—can you think of ways to share these interests with the class, to involve the children in them? The topic isn't as important as the depth of interest and knowledge a teacher has in something that stimulates and engages children.

Mimi is a joyful, fun-loving person. She picks up on the fun her children have and expands it into curriculum: they're running when she has planned a circle game, so she encourages their running, racing, thundering, pound-

✳ **x** ✳

ing across the pavement, laughing, and giggling till they collapse in a heap at her feet—and *then* comes the circle game. Not all of us are as ebullient and flexible as Mimi Chenfeld, but each and every teacher can see when children are having fun or think something is funny and can provide leeway to build on it, playfully guiding the group back on track after the fun has been explored.

The two extraordinary things about Mimi Chenfeld are (1) that she's this completely original force of nature called Mimi Chenfeld, and (2) that she shares this warm, gleeful, life-relishing self with the children and teachers she works with. We can't be Mimi Chenfeld, but each of us has a *self* that is unique and full of creative and wonderful qualities in its own right. Which means all of us can make it a goal to spontaneously share more of who *we* truly are with the children we teach. No doubt flat, paper-doll teachers can teach, but authentic people can teach more effectively. Read this collection of Mimi-isms, and may her spirit inspire you!

—Polly Greenberg

Polly Greenberg was the editor of NAEYC's professional journal, Young Children, *for fifteen years and, for seven of those years, the editor of books published by NAEYC. Among her own published articles and books is* The Devil Has Slippery Shoes: A Biased Biography of the Child Development Group of Mississippi, *a widely acclaimed chronicle of Mississippi's famous Head Start program.*

Dear Mimi,

Thank you for coming to visit us. I really enjoy the fun we that we had with each other I am a very shy person, but could tell your not. It's fun having you here. OH I for- got tell you that you are a very very nice firend because I think you are playfull.

From Your
Friend,
usaphea En

Introduction:

My Next Fifty Years

HELLO
Mimi

For weeks in my sixteenth summer I worked as a sales clerk at Loft's Candy Store. I was fired because I couldn't wrap! (Nowadays I'm better at rapping!) Those two weeks were the only in my entire work life that I wasn't with children or involved with issues concerning children. (Imagine if I *had* been able to wrap!)

The following summer, my friend Rhoda and I were counselors at a sleepaway camp, Jekoce, an hour out of New York City. We had the "baby bunk": our campers were the infants and toddlers of senior counselors and other camp staff. I've always loved babies, but the summer I spent hanging out with those smart, honest, creative, hilarious little ones clinched my lifelong love affair with our youngest learners. Today, with all-day, five-day-a-week programs for our newest students, I'm still totally filled with awe, delight, respect, and feelings of responsibility to preserve the sacred spirits of those youngest members of our human family. When people ask me how long I've been teaching movement, dance, and rhythms to young children, I tell them, "I have never taught one child how to move or dance! My claim to fame is moving, dancing, laughing, and celebrating with them! They already know!"

When I began teaching in 1956, my room was a stage in an old, worn country school ten miles and ten light-years away from New York's capital city. That year New York State was caught in the traumatic changes of central-izing small districts into larger, combined districts. There was also a serious shortage of teachers and classrooms in the country. With no walls, thick theatrical curtains, and weird lights, my fourth-grade "classroom" was a place without specialists, lunches off, or bathroom breaks for teachers. I was the young, new, off-the-wall teacher on a staff of strict, linear, veteran teachers whose welcome to me was, let's say, tepid! That trial-by-fire year I learned many lessons. The most important lesson: *I had to be myself!* No matter what the pressures pushing conformity, inhibiting spirit, or squelching creativity, I had to be true to what I believed was right for the children. Long before Howard Gardner's multiple intelligences theory, I ener-gized my basic texts with dance, laughter, improvisation, and hands-on activities.

A few years ago a call came in from a man who was once a boy in that fourth grade so long ago. Now a grand-father, he had come across one of my books and tracked me down. We talked for an hour. He remembered things I had totally forgotten. What hit me most about that special conversation was his saying, "Mimi, do you know what I remember most clearly from that year?" Without hesitating, he continued, "You read us stories from *Winnie the Pooh* and we danced!"

That first year I had a sad little girl, Agnes. She was mopey and quiet and could easily get lost in the dynamics of the day. One early autumn afternoon we were out in the field playing ball. I was pitching. I noticed Agnes sitting under a tree, her head down, her shoulders slumped. I yelled, "Time out!" and ran over to her. She was crying as if her heart would break. *What's the matter?* Under my eyes, which I'd always thought of as clear and true-sighted, she'd been left out of games and friendships by cliques that had formed in the classes. How could I have missed such an unacceptable situation? I was in shock! Upset at myself for not seeing what was now obvious, furious at the kids for alienating one of their classmates, and devastated at Agnes' loneliness and rejection, I stopped the game, called the kids over, and told them to look at Agnes and tell me why she was crying. I couldn't go on with class work until this was resolved, so we sat under the tree for the rest of the afternoon. We talked, we all cried, and when it was over, we made promises never to let a child be hurt in our "family."

I knew then and I know now how easy it is for kids to gang up, bully, form tightly knit cliques, and leave others out, and I know too well how easy it is for teachers to miss such goings-on. I urge every adult in any relationship with children to treat these tragic situations as *emergency* scenarios that must be attended to immediately! When one child suffers from bullying, when one child is left out or put down, *everyone* is hurt and the spirit of the group is destroyed. The safety net is torn, and we all fall through!

That first teaching year I wore a black-and-white tweed winter coat with a fake white fur collar that draped around the shoulders. After the Agnes crisis and resolution we'd become a hugging, affectionate, loving family group. During recess, welcomes, and farewells, even the boys got their hugs from me. (We had so much fun! Many of the kids hated weekends and played healthy when they were sick in order not to miss school.) During winter break I took my coat to the dry cleaner. I hadn't noticed that the white on the fake fur collar was now a strange grayish color. The counter person asked, "What happened to your coat?" We figured out there was only one explanation: months' worth of small faces rubbing against the collar as we hugged our morning hellos, during recesses, and our afternoon good-byes! The dry cleaner concluded that the collar was so discolored, it could not be cleaned. He recommended it be cut off and a narrower throat collar redesigned and sewn. Which it was! I can still see that coat collar with the stamp of the children's faces deep in its fake fur!

The poet Theodore Roethke reminds us that teaching is "one of the few professions that permits love." For fifty years I have suggested to education students and in-service teachers, "If you don't *love* the children, do, for their sake and yours, consider a career change!" I wish I had kept that collar.

My husband's favorite hobby is magic. He always

attends an annual magicians' convention in Columbus, and I get to enjoy the big magic show on Friday night. That show occurs the night before our Columbus Association for the Education of Young Children's annual spring conference. One year, as I was being blown away by the spectacular, logic-defying tricks *(How did they do that?)*, I thought ahead to the CAEYC conference scheduled for the following day. While doves flew out of magicians' empty hands and colorful scarves appeared out of thin air, I couldn't help thinking of my talented, dedicated colleagues readying for our annual get-together. I thought of the magic in *their* hands, the amazing, mind-boggling, heartstring-plucking tricks of the trade that *those* magicians performed every day, to rare applause:

* welcoming children who know no English and helping them learn their new language while respecting their native tongue;
* reassuring crying, clinging toddlers that they are in a safe place;
* comforting children afraid to try, that they may find the courage to try;
* guiding children who never play with others to reach out and touch another hand.

I am proud to call these magic-makers my friends and colleagues.

This past year our Ohio Association for the Education of Young Children (OAEYC) shared the convention center with a national cheerleaders' gathering. Brightly colored, pom-pom-waving, glittering cheerleading groups of all ages, from all over the country, packed the vast halls and corridors.

Their drills and chants throbbed to the beat of spectacular percussive choreographies. As I made my way through their lively teams to pick up a quick lunch at the food court, it hit me! On one side of the building, two thousand early childhood professionals gathered for workshops, presentations, and exhibits. On the other side, cheerleading teams juggled, shouted, and somersaulted in fierce competition. But who were the *real* cheerleaders? I vote for our teachers, administrators, assistants, and aides, who were:

* stuffing their bags with puppets, pop-up books, handouts, and giveaways from exhibitors' booths to help their kids;
* jotting down fresh ideas to enhance learning;
* discovering new projects and activities with which to delight their students;
* inspiring, motivating, delighting, and cheering each other on to become lifelong learners on this amazing journey of ours.

We are the *real* cheerleaders, using basic props that no catalog sells: smiles, loving voices, warm hearts, open minds, clapping hands, hugging arms, and endless words of support and encouragement. In our gatherings we rediscover that we are all winners!

Michelangelo's motto, "I am still learning," is so on target! No matter what our subject areas, grade levels, or students' ages, we learn as we teach every day! Over the years I've spent treasured times with children from infancy to adolescence, from Head Start to Upward Bound, from kindergarten to high school, with children trying to get by in homeless shelters to more fortunate children who go home to loving families in nice houses. With *all* those students, I have found ways to play with ideas that delight and intrigue me.

Many of the ideas (the best ideas) come *from* the kids! And wherever it comes from, an idea is a good idea if *you* like it! If you don't like it, you probably shouldn't try it—unless, of course, it's a required part of your center's curriculum. The challenge is to find imaginative ways to enrich that idea. An idea has its own life, and the fun of creative teaching is messing around with ideas until they take flight. Unfortunately, this stressed-out, tested-out time we live in leaves some teachers and students little opportunity to celebrate and explore all the dimensions of their original ideas in order to fully experience the joy of learning! Our courageous, imaginative, confident, fiercely independent, knowledgeable, and gifted teachers can take heart from their sisters and brothers who kept learning alive during the darkest times in history—slavery, war, Holocaust, famine, and natural disaster, to name a few tragic chapters in the human story.

My metaphors help keep me strong! My house of beliefs is built of bricks! No wolf can blow it down. I am spinning and twirling as we all are, but I keep my balance because while I spin, I spot. That spot is the center of it all—*the children*! Once we take our focus off the children, we are caught in the spinning and we all fall down.

Too many excellent teachers of all grades and of all ages are leaving education. This difficult time for our very special family—those who are called to this sacred field because they want to be with children in healthy, helpful, connecting, and inspiring ways—has been painfully challenging. Sadly, when teachers look around and see what appears to be a growing number of decision makers in our society who do not honor research findings, who do not honor principles of developmentally appropriate practices, many head to the EXIT door. But teachers who stay, who keep the faith, who keep the children at the center of their focus, are like the heroes and heroines of history who walked along with the children, even through thickest darkness.

My journey into the next fifty years has already begun! In my backpack for the adventure I carry my puppet, Snowball, my tambourine, all my songs, a purple scarf to remind me of our magic, a pom-pom to remind me that we are the best cheerleaders, and the clear memory of a much-hugged fake fur collar on a long-ago black-and-white tweed coat. When I think of the collar, I remember that love and kindness must be the air that sweetens our learning.

I should have kept that collar!

Snowball

I am just bursting to tell you about the puppet in my life, Snowball, a little brown-and-white, floppy-eared puppy puppet. Many years ago, the white part of his fur was brilliant white. It now borders on beige!

Snowball has an accumulation of years and years of children's germs, tears, fingerprints, sniffles, dribbles, whispers, clutches, hugs, tugs, and kisses on him. If you touch him, you'll be immune to whatever bug is going around. When he retires (which will not be in the foreseeable future), I'll donate him to the National Institutes of Health so they can use him for research on immunization. I'm sure he carries the cures to most of our dread diseases on his furry little paws, ears, and nose.

Snowball does not talk out loud. If he did, he'd sound like he was from the Bronx, as I do, and the children don't need two New York City accents in their delicate Midwestern ears. Snowball whispers to me, and I tell the children what he says. His communication with them may be nonverbal, but it is crystal clear.

Over the years,

* lonely children who never talked to anyone talked to Snowball;
* children who needed special cheering, TLC, reassurance, and comfort received those gifts in abundance from Snowball;
* unfriendly, troubled children stopped their aggressive behavior immediately when Snowball let them know their negative actions hurt his feelings;
* children who were rarely noticed by their peers were always noticed by Snowball.

Thousands of children (including folks who were once children) can list more reasons for loving Snowball than did Elizabeth Barrett Browning when she wrote of her love for Robert. Here is just a smattering of children's accolades for their special little friend:

* "He's such a good listener."
* "He's cute!"
* "He always cares about us and likes to be with us."
* "Even though he makes hundreds of mistakes, he keeps trying and he's not ashamed if he goofs up."

* "He never, never leaves anyone out. If some-
  one feels sick or sad, he has extra kisses and
  hugs and makes them feel better."
* "He's sad when we're sad."
* "He's cuddly."
* "He's funny."
* "He's lovable."
* "We tell him secrets."
* "He does good tricks, like 'If you're happy
  and you know it waggle your ears.' He's so
  silly."
* "If someone's mad he makes them laugh."
* "He's extra nice to new kids so they don't
  feel shy."

In our creative-movement sessions with children, Snowball's participation is minimal in time but maximal (is this
a word? I like it) in quality. He shows up only during the
last few minutes of our classes, sending the children off
with good-bye kisses.

Once we had a three-and-a-half-year-old boy, Jim,
who was (and is) deaf. For weeks, he sat and watched our
stories and dances but did not participate. One day when
Snowball was kissing the kids good-bye, Jim beckoned to
me from his spot on the sidelines, gesturing that Snowball
had forgotten to kiss one of the children. I thanked Jim
and quickly remedied the situation. At that time (and to
this day), Snowball was called on to do his favorite trick,
the peek-a-boo trick, which he never got right. We always
showed Snowball how to do it, covering up our faces with

our hands and repeating the chant, "Where are the kids?" three times before we revealed our peek-a-boo faces. *Ta da!* But Snowball, the slow learner, just couldn't get it. (And he still can't.) We kept coaching him to keep his furry little face hidden behind his furry little paws while we chanted three times, "Where's Snowball?" but he always popped out on the count of one. This quirk kept the children in gales of laughter. I would say, "Shall we give him another chance?" Once a child giggled, "Let's give him a million chances!"

Well, back to our friend Jim, who had never uttered a single sound in his almost four years of living. His regular sessions at speech therapy were to no avail. No one had ever heard his voice. Can you guess what Jim's first spoken words were? You guessed it! "Where's Snowball?"

Early childhood professionals are grossly underpaid, but they are real pros. For example, they try not to cry in front of the children. That unforgettable day, we waited until the children departed for home before we permitted our tears to flow.

Snowball has been invited to more parties, sleepovers, suppers, picnics, trips, and holiday get-togethers than most humans on the planet. One day one of our early childhood classes made cookies. As I watched the children mix the dough, taking turns shaking in the sugar and sprinkling in the flavor, I felt a tug at my sleeve. Ezra, a strong, muscular boy, had a great idea. "Mim, why don't you go and get Snowball so he can join us for cookies?"

Snowball's magic is not limited to young children. Some years ago I taught one of those total immersion weekend in-service courses for teachers called "More Fun

Than a Field Trip: Teaching in the Key of Life." Snowball and I welcomed the participants at the doorway. Most of them smiled or waved to Snowball as they came in and found their seats. One gentleman arrived with a puzzled, hesitant expression on his face and a reluctant rhythm in his walk. He was a high school athletic coach and science teacher. When Snowball waved to him in greeting, the burly coach took a giant step back and threw me a disgusted, skeptical look. I knew he was thinking, "What the heck did I sign up for?"

We had to give him an A for effort. He stuck with our often off-the-wall antics for fifteen solid hours! At the close of the course, people departed with warm farewells and new friendships. Our tough high school coach/science teacher paused at the doorway, patted Snowball on the head, and said, "Bye, buddy!"

Summers, when my husband and I relax at the community center swimming pool, children of all ages ask, "Where's Snowball?" When I walk through shopping malls, arts festivals, powwows, and airport terminals, children (and alumni who were once children) stop me and ask, "How's Snowball?"

Funny how a little brown-and-white (beige), worn but warm puppy puppet can be so memorable to so many people. Maybe we need Snowball to remind us that our children are longing for friends—human, animal, puppet—who:

* are good listeners;
* never leave anyone out;

* make them laugh;
* cheer them on;
* always have extra kisses and hugs to make
  them feel better when they're sick or sad;
* can be trusted;
* love them (no matter what).

I've learned a lot from Snowball!

My Puppet Is on Ritalin

Snowball, my "main squeeze" little brown-and-white puppy puppet, has accumulated thousands of frequent-flier miles in our travels around the country hanging out with teachers and kids of all ages. Wherever we go, he's a hit!

In our movement/music/story times at the Leo Yassenoff Jewish Community Center in Columbus, Ohio, where I've worked since 1970, Snowball sometimes makes an appearance and tells me (in my ear only; only I can hear him!) his favorite part of the story or idea we just celebrated. I tell the kids what he says. For example, if we create a story/dance for "Goldilocks and the Three Bears," Snowball might tell me his favorite part of the story was when the wolf huffed and puffed but couldn't blow the house down! He *always* goofs it up! He is courteous, sweet-tempered, and interested, but he just doesn't pay attention! He's easily distracted! Even blanket-hugging homesick toddlers burst into peals of laughter at some of his off-the-wall responses. They love him and love to correct him!

"Snowball," they cheerily scold, *"Pay attention!"*

On other occasions, in his role as a member of the "Medical Emergency Squad," Snowball rushes in to aid a fallen child.

"Where does it hurt?" I ask.

The usually *not* hurt but startled kid will point to an arm or a leg.

"Snowball, will you kiss Tyler's boo-boo?" I prescribe.

Snowball to the rescue! Mushy kisses go on Tyler's nose or the top of his head, while tears dry and are replaced by giggles, Tyler corrects the medic.

"No, Snowball! *Not* my head! My leg! Pay attention!"

One treatment from Snowball and most injuries are immediately healed.

When a more reluctant class comes into our space (kids get into moods, too, right?), I call Snowball to help motivate the group into action.

Snowball whispers into my ear. I convey the message.

"Hey, friends, Snowball doesn't think you guys are in great shape today. I told him you were high jumpers and fast runners, but he doesn't believe me! Shall we show him?"

"Okay!" More than okay! Our droopy-eyed slouchers straighten up and take off (always around the room and in the same direction). Music *on*! Any rhythmic music from *anywhere* in the world will do. Round and round the room they run.

"Put the music in your feet," I call. We run run run then we jump jump jump. Run run run jump jump jump until we all fall down!

While the kids lie on the floor catching their breath, I ask Snowball, "What do you think of our super-fit-as-a-fiddle kids now?"

Snowball flops his ears and claps his paws in glee, full of excitement. Then he whispers in my ear. I tell the children, "Snowball says that was so cool. Can you do it again?"

The pooped-out children, still catching their breath, shout, *"No way!"*

"We're tired and ready for a story," Jake explains.

I lower my voice in confidence to the group. "You know how eager and excited, how hyper, Snowball is? Should we do our whole running and jumping exercise for him again?"

"Snowball, I think you should be on Ritalin!" Evan advises. While his classmates agree, Snowball bounces, wiggles, and flops his ears.

"I think he's so excited and happy to be with you today," I say, offering my opinion.

The kids chime in to tell about friends and family members on medication!

We dance and sing our story, and when we say good-bye, Snowball reappears and gives good-bye kisses. Now these are four- and four-and-a-half-year-olds, many of whom have known Snowball from their early childhood education programs in infant and toddler groups. This day, Audrey runs back to share a momentous discovery she just made.

"Mimi, it seems that Snowball is a puppet!"

Between waves of laughter I reassure her, "He is a puppet, honey!"

Looking at him meaningfully for a second, she hugs him, gives him a sweet good-bye kiss, and runs to catch up with her class.

We have an appointment at the doctor's. Snowball will probably have to be tested. Unfocused, silly random responses, overly enthusiastic behavior, not recognizing limits, and confusing comprehension can mean only one course—medication!

We might have to go for a second opinion!

People whose sweater sleeves aren't pulled out of shape by small, fingerpainted, sweaty hands; whose faces aren't smudged from kisses pressed by tiny lips smeared with colored markers; who don't cut their companions' food into bite-sized portions at gala dinner parties; who don't go on road trips and shout, "Look, everyone! Cows! How many cows do you see?"; whose efficiently structured daily lives are filled with mature conversations and activities often ask me, "Why do you hang out with young children?" Sometimes I flip them an answer like "Because they're there." Sometimes I shrug and give an answer like "Just lucky, I guess." Sometimes I laugh. "Darned if I know," I say.

But I really do know. I hang out with young people because *I have to!*

In this shook-up, fast-lane, topsy-turvy, high-tech whirl of a world, where cool is hot and yes is no, where violence is epidemic and the lessons of history aren't learned, being with young children is like aerobics for the imagination, nourishment for the spirit. Sharing time with young children is like a splash in a deliciously cold, energizing lake on a smoggy, muggy day. The honesty of young children is startling.

My friend, six-year-old Maria, looked at my naked face with her clear eyes and asked, "Mimi, why are you so old?" Before I could answer, she took my hand and in a worried voice said, "I hope you don't die."

Being with children is a matter of life and death! It takes courage to spend time with young children. It takes a tough skin and a mushy heart. Young children keep me honest and brave.

In this crazy world of stereotyped thinking, of mass-media images and trite phrases, young children demonstrate originality as they share their love affair with language, with life.

When Brian announced he'd lost his first tooth, I asked him what he'd done with it.

"Put it under my pillow."

"What did you get?"

"I got a dollar!"

"Who gave you the dollar?"

"The Truth Fairy!"

Creative problem solving in their expanding worlds is native to young children. Jackie, another first-tooth loser, was excited as she told me about how her tooth fell out.

"Did you hide it under your pillow?" I asked in the familiar litany.

Jackie's voice dropped to barely a whisper. "No," she confided.

"Oh, why not, honey?"

"I didn't want the Tooth Fairy to come into my room."

"So, what did you do?"

"I put my tooth on the top step of the stairs."

"Did the Tooth Fairy leave you anything?"

"Yes!" she exclaimed happily. "She left a quarter on the step!"

Young children remind us that the world is new and belongs to them. They own the moon, the sun, the stars, the songs.

Grandpa Joe was singing "Old MacDonald" to his two-year-old friend Pnina.

"No, Grandpa Joe. No!" Pnina tried to shush him.

Grandpa Joe stopped singing. Pnina wagged her finger at him.

"No! Grandpa Joe, Pnina's 'Old MacDonald Had a Farm!' *My song!*"

Why do I hang out with young children? Because being with young children is a lesson in loving. In our statistical society, where feelings are hoarded, measured, metered, and splintered, we learn about wholeness.

Four-year-old Oren's mom watched in shock from the kitchen window as Oren picked every flower in the garden. He ran to the back door, presenting his treasure to her.

"These are for you, Mommy."

"Oren, one flower would have been enough for me. You didn't have to pick all the flowers!"

"No, Mommy," the little boy explained. "I love you too much for just one flower. I love you more than all the flowers!"

Young children keep us from getting stuck in neutral. They make us drive in the center lane of life.

With young children, we are always connected to amazement. They faze us!

I was sitting with a few young children around a library table, talking about their favorite kinds of clothing. I was taking notes because these were interviews for my textbook, then in progress.

As they shared their opinions about styles and colors, they moved closer to me. The smallest child settled in my lap. My pen scribbled along with their conversation about Sunday clothes, sandals, blue jeans, Mickey Mouse T-shirts. In the midst of the lively exchange, five-year-old Aleah looked at me with wide eyes and asked, "Mimi, do spiderwebs ever wake you up?"

I spend time with young children so that I can be continually astonished. Their observations delight and inspire me. Their questions challenge me to face my own immense ignorance.

When I'm with young children, I wish on Twinkle, Twinkle, Little Star, I clap for Tinker Bell, I cry for Charlotte, I brake for beauty, I notice a single ant climbing a blade of grass, I grow toward the light.

The magical wisdom of young children is contagious.

I was explaining to the three- and four-year-olds on the last day of preschool that my little puppy puppet, Snowball, was going to Peek-a-Boo Summer Camp so he could keep practicing the peek-a-boo trick, because he couldn't ever get it right. Some of the children smiled and said, "We're going to camp too." A few just looked and nodded. The older, more sophisticated four-year-olds watched me with X-ray eyes.

Know-it-all Brett challenged me: "He's really a puppet, isn't he?"

"Yes, of course he is."

Brett pondered for a few seconds, then came over and kissed the little peek-a-boo student. "Have a good time in camp, Snowball!"

Why do I hang out with young children? Because in all my years, no one had ever before asked me the answer-defying question, "Do spiderwebs ever wake you up?"

(And how are we helping our children keep the wonder?)

Dear Mrs. Chenfeld

I Like what we did today.
It was fun. I wanted to be bu
author but I don't think I'll go
though because I'm very poor.
I Like you very much

Your
friend

Jana
Stewart

I
Like
you
you
got
Class

$E = MC^2$

Under the ABCs of *Anxiety, Betterment,* and *Competition,* many adults practice a kind of push-comes-to-shove child-rearing philosophy that starts programming children for success at birth or, sometimes, even in the womb.

"To everything there is a season" takes on new relevance as we view the disturbing educational approach that boasts of four-year-olds naming characters from Shakespeare before learning to love the rhymes and rhythms of Mother Goose, that encourages children to skip by "Twinkle, Twinkle, Little Star" and move directly to Beethoven's Ninth. These well-intentioned but misguided parents and teachers forget that children find their own ten toes without the aid of cards flashing pictures of ten toes. They crawl without crawling lessons, and babble, imitate, sing, and talk without the assistance of computer games.

Parents and teachers who advocate for this speeded-up, adult-directed curriculum often look to such geniuses as Michelangelo, Einstein, and Leonardo as role models. Let's take a closer look at those lives: Michelangelo's parents never encouraged his artistic abilities. Einstein was considered a slow learner. Leonardo spent his life looking for the mother he never knew, achieving his phenomenal accomplishments without strong parental direction. I'm not recommending discouragement, desertion, or misunderstanding as guarantees of high-achieving offspring! I'm just reminding everyone that children are complex, total beings (in the state of becoming, as we all are). Children begin the world anew with their own unique combination of strengths, interests, originality, courage, imagination, and determination. They are not "little sponges," as one new-age parent described them in a magazine article.

The most distressing aspect of a high-pressure educational philosophy is that it conveys a closed-up notion of the world. Parents and teachers who practice it are really sending children these messages:

* We will provide you with all the answers.
* Learn them and you will succeed.
* Learn them faster and you will make it sooner than everyone else.

(Why, these children may even hit puberty before kindergarten!)

In an unnatural, anxiety-riddled setting, there's no room for questions, spontaneous discovery, the surprise of exploration, or the excitement of learning. It's the product that is emphasized; the process is devalued. Plato believed "the beginning of learning is wonder." Where does wonder fit into an accelerated, pressure-cooker scheme?

Children are the greatest learners on earth. They can learn anything, in any way, from anyone. But just what is it children are learning?

I'm afraid many "superbabies" are learning how not to be children. They are learning before they need to and more than they need to about tension, competition, failure, disappointment, and frustration. Most important, they may be learning that love is connected somehow to successfully performing for parents and teachers. Children who lose their spirit of adventure, their willingness to risk new experiences, or their ability to play with ideas and concepts may be considered deprived, maybe even disabled.

I'm worried about our children caught in this acceleration process. Two incidents chosen from a too-ample supply are:

1. As his fellow kindergartners practice writing their names with feelings of exuberance and pride, Robbie freezes at the touch of a pencil in his hand, terrified to write even his own name for fear of making a mistake. Do you think Robbie enjoys his lessons?

2. Every day, first-grader Sherry shreds her school papers, calling herself dumb and stupid. Instead of heeding A. A. Milne's glorious proclamation—"But now I am Six, I'm clever as clever. / So I think I'll be six now for ever

and ever."—she stares with deep, sorrowful, defeated six-year-old eyes full of failure and says, "I wish I was dead." Does Sherry "rejoice in her own works"?

I've seen kindergarten children sit in silent reading groups working on worksheets. I've seen three-year-olds be told to redo their Thanksgiving pictures and to "Do it right! Pilgrims' hats are *black;* don't use any other color. Watch Nancy; she's doing the *best* job!"

When teachers and parents discuss ways to enrich the lives of young children—ways to help them to *learn to love learning*—the best suggestions are the oldest, most natural, most obvious, most simple. They are so easy that we forget we already know them:

* Hang loose and relax.
* Talk with your children. Share and compare observations, questions, experiences, wishes, wondering. Laugh together.
* Listen to music of all kinds. Enjoy the music. Let it inspire movement, art, stories, quiet times.
* Read to and with your children. Surround them with stories, poems, riddles, plays. Read to yourself. (What books do *you* love? If you want children to love reading, show them by your example.) Discover the delight of creating your own stories, your own writings. Children already know about this. Keep the flame burning.

* Walk with the children. Walk with awareness. Stop! Look! Listen! Be a person on whom nothing is lost. Martin Buber believed that everything is waiting to be hallowed by you. What do you hallow? A walk around the street with an aware, responsive, sensitive, involved adult is more enjoyable and valuable to a child than a trip around the world with a rigid, closed-minded, authoritarian tour leader.

* Encourage imaginative responses, original thinking, freedom of expression, and new experiences. Don't be a critic or a judge. Be a person who rejoices in your own works and the works of others.

* Use the resources at your doorstep: libraries, museums, art galleries, parks, playgrounds, construction sites, gardens, zoos, bakeries, fruit stands, orchards, street signs, parking lots. The word *boring* does not belong in the vocabulary of any child.

Our kids don't need expensive gimmicks, shiny educational tools, designer jigsaw puzzles, video games, and heavy-handed adult intervention in their daily education. Let's not rely only on technology, no matter how great its potential in the learning process. Our children need an environment sweetened with tender, loving care, encouragement, inspiration, role models, and time—time to play, pretend, explore, experiment, and wonder; time to develop at their own pace and in their own special rhythms. When children learn in safe, supportive settings under the gentle, constant guidance of loving adults, they prove over and over again that they are among the most creative members of this gifted and talented human family of ours.

Be ready for astonishment. Those of us who have spent most of our lives working with children know that when we let them, *they teach us* about looking at everyday, ordinary miracles with fresh eyesight and insight. Children take us on a journey to our own beginnings, when the world was new and waiting to be discovered again.

We have a lot to learn.

Lisa is ten. We're driving together on a Saturday afternoon and talking about the wonderful computer in her classroom.

"It can do everything! It has so much power! It's so much fun!" She loves that computer.

I'm honest about my feelings. I tell her I believe in the power of good teachers, not machines. Do computers have laps? Can computers hug? Do computers have shoulders to cry on? When do computers surprise us with spontaneous, unsolicited ideas?

I ask Lisa, "Which would you rather have? An interesting, challenging, exciting teacher or your computer?" She answers without hesitation, "I'd rather have my computer than my teacher."

I am stunned. "Why?"

"Well, the computer is . . ." She searches for words, the right word. "The computer is warm."

"*Warm?*" I am shouting.

"Yeah, the computer is warm and my teacher is . . ." She narrows her eyes and adds, *"cold."*

I am speechless.

"The computer," she continues, "is *comforting.* It's *encouraging.* If you make a mistake, it says, 'Try again,' or 'Better luck next time.' If you get it right, it says, 'Good job,' or 'Fine job!' My teacher never tells us we've done well. She's never satisfied. We're never good enough for her. She never gives us words of praise. No matter how great we do, she never tells us she's pleased."

As we drive along, I admit to myself that given the choice between a machine programmed to be comforting, warm, and encouraging and a teacher who programs herself to be negative, discouraging, and cold, I, too, would choose the machine!

Lisa's confession haunts me. At home I walk our dogs and meet almost-three-year-old Tia at the peak of celebrating her very first success at skipping. We cheer for her. "Yaaaaay! Right on! Super skipper!" We applaud, smile, hug. Tia skips down the driveway, eyes shining with pride and accomplishment. I remember Tia's milestones: her first walking, her first talking, and now her first skipping. Each stage was accompanied by affectionate encouragement and praise from family and friends.

When does the celebrating of learning stop?

Lisa's feelings about the warmth of her computer and the coldness of her teacher continue to obsess me. I think about seven-year-old Andrew, who rushed excitedly into his house one day after school.

"Mom," he called. "We have a new teacher—the best, the very best teacher I've ever had!"

"But I thought you liked your other teacher," Andrew's mother wondered.

"I do, but our new teacher is the best. Our other teacher said, *'No, No, No,'* and our new teacher says, *'Yes! Yes! Yes!'"*

Language is the core, the key, the foundation of every class, subject, activity, and relationship. I should say *languages:* the language of textbooks, printed materials, and curriculum resources; the language of daily events—the give-and-take, instructions, directions, announcements, reactions, questions, and conversations; the language of feelings—the life and death of the spirit conveyed through verbal and nonverbal communication. A teacher's language holds the power to help children learn and grow together or, when it conveys negatives—"You're dumb!" "Look at those mistakes!" "This work isn't good."—to shrink their spirits.

Are you a *Yes* teacher or a *No* teacher? A vote for *life*—for *Yes*—yields immeasurable rewards. A vote for *No* has dire implications. Read on!

The first graders were instructed to make a clock and to be sure all the numbers for the hours were written clearly. Katy jumped into the assignment with enthusiasm. She carefully wrote the twelve numbers of the clock on a round paper plate. They were perfect and so beautiful that she was inspired to decorate each number with a tiny flower surrounding it. She hurried to school with her colorful clock held in her hands like an offering.

A different child returned home from school that day. Back slumped, head bent, eyes down, Katy opened the door.

"Did your teacher like your clock, Katy?" her mother asked eagerly.

Without a word, Katy dropped the clock on the floor. Her mother picked it up. Across the face of the clock, scratched so deeply it tore the paper, was a huge X and, in angry handwriting, the teacher's message: "Did not follow instructions!"

When does the celebration of learning stop?

There is an old Yiddish custom. When young children completed a page of study, their teacher dropped a dot of honey on the bottom of the page. The children were encouraged to dip their fingers in the honey and taste its sweetness. Learning should always be sweet!

I shared this custom with teachers at a workshop. One of the participants couldn't contain herself and related this story. That very week, her own first grader brought home a paper. There, on the top of Jeff's paper, his teacher had pasted a sad face with teardrops flowing from the eyes down the entire length of the paper. At the bottom, next to the stream of tears, was clearly printed: "I am very disappointed in your work."

When Lisa, Tia, Andrew, Katy, and Jeff come to your class, what will they find? Who will they find?

Will they find a teacher who is "user-friendly"?

Will they find a teacher programmed to be comforting, warm, and encouraging?

Will the language of the classroom be *Yes*?

Will you spin words of praise, drop honey on the page, and say in everything you do, "The celebrating of learning never stops"?

Say *Yes*!

Dear Mimi,

Before you came I was so exicted. When you first walked in the door I thought to myself you looked like a Indian.

I had so much fun when were warming up. I like you alot I can't wait you to come back" Plus I Love the way you talk to us

A Letter to Families and Friends of the Children in Room 13

Thank you for responding to our call for scrounge items. When you come to the open house next week, you'll notice that our huge basket of stuff is almost empty! Look for former contents in our homemade instruments, inventions, puzzles, museum exhibits, collections, and constructions, and in our imaginative sculpture show in the gallery area. Amazing what our talented kindergarten artists and scholars can create from your cereal boxes, egg crates, coffee cans, toilet paper and paper towel rolls, clear plastic boxes, and fast-food Styrofoam containers. Please keep these excellent materials coming in, as we have many more things we can do with them, always. The children are becoming more aware of how often we just toss away such valuable materials, so our scrounge works to help our environment.

Thanks for answering the survey we sent out during the first week of school asking you to jot down any areas of your experience you're willing to share with the children. We've already welcomed three honored guests and learned a lot from them:

* Adam's grandfather told us about his work as a school custodian. The children listened intently as he talked about all the things he has to do to keep a school running smoothly and safely. They asked some very thoughtful questions.
* Anthony's aunt taught the kids how to design and make lovely bead patterns and introduced them to braiding. Marvelous for small- and gross-motor skills. (And for counting, colors, and sorting.)
* Destiny's mom told us about her job working in the housewares department of a big department store. The children loved the catalogs she shared and were fascinated by all the different household items and appliances she knew about.

Of course, all of our classroom guests received beautifully written and illustrated thank-you letters from each child.

Now, about Our Place. Some of you have expressed concern that the kindergartners in room 9 down the hall seem to be more focused on practicing basic skills than our children here in room 13. You were impressed with their seatwork, paperwork, and structured lessons. We respect the different ways children learn in our school, and we are eager to tell you about the developmentally appropriate practices approach we share with your children in Our Place. We deeply believe that the students in room 13 are learning their basic skills, but in diverse ways, which we will try to describe and which you'll have the chance to see for yourselves at the open house next week (or anytime you care to visit us—you're always welcome).

You may notice our room is a bit cluttered! So much is happening here that sometimes it's impossible to get organized and neat (even for the open house).

Our dress-up center is very popular (thanks to you folks who sent in the clothing—the children love it). Our M. N. M. trio (Monte, Nicole, and Michele) is deeply into playing with their costumes first thing every morning. You can't imagine all the oral language, vocabulary, listening skills, and social development that grow with dress-up dramas!

You'll understand why we advocated for keeping our sandbox when you see how most of the children enjoy it. We think they must be the descendants of desert people! Especially Tiffany and Juan, who lead the group to the sand every free-activity time. Among their numerous projects are the building of tunnels, cities, and sandscapes and the discovering of buried treasures (they love playing archaeologists). Last week Latia joined in and surprised everyone by writing the whole alphabet in the sand. We called it *sandmanship.* The children learn so much about measuring—cups, pints, quarts, gallons—in their world of sand.

Be careful when you stop at the inventions lab. Lamar and Jennifer are deep at work on a very intricate invention-in-progress. We can't wait for them to introduce it and explain it to us. Remember, these scientific breakthroughs take time, so we have to be patient. A lot of problem solving, decision making, and cooperative learning go into invention. They promised to try to finish it in time for our science fair (which you will learn about soon).

Have the children told you about their fabulous musical instruments? They're constructed of and decorated with scrounge and found objects, in colorful and original ways. Every day we use our instruments for stories, parades, sound effects, math, science, and special events. In our weather study, we composed a blustery thunderstorm symphony. We enriched our math lesson by adding the sound of one instrument at a time until we could hear the sum of all the parts. Then we subtracted one after another until we had silence—zero. We like to compose rhythms using numbers and patterns. Of course, we can't help dancing to our wonderful music! You would too! We often write down our choreography. For example, ten jumps, five kicks, ten jumping claps, two wiggle-wiggles, repeat. Easy to follow and so much fun to do. If we have time, we'll demonstrate at the open house.

Room 13 is drenched in language! Words! Posters! Signs! Charts! Cartoon labels! Letters! Our word wall is packed with words the children suggest and recognize.

Doesn't it make great wallpaper? The class rules prominently posted on the door were discussed and agreed upon by the children. Our mailbox is bursting with mail, which gets delivered every day. It takes time to help the children write and read their letters. Their letter and word recognition and comprehension are strengthened every day in everything we do. Notice the postage stamps the children designed. They love to get mail!

The orange flipchart near the nature table is our songbook. Look through its large, bright pages. Read the words to all the songs your children know. Remember, the music teacher is on maternity leave, but we sing every day anyway. The children recognize every song and follow the words as we sing. Is this singing or reading? (We say it's both!) We love the illustrations the children designed for each song.

Reading is happening all the time in Our Place. We don't limit reading to one specific time slot. We're almost finished with the Ananci stories. We read a story or poem every day after lunch. Our nature-loving students are immersed in books about butterflies, dinosaurs, fish, and volcanoes. All the children are fascinated by the variations of the Cinderella story told by people around the world. Even though the holidays are still far off, the children want to hear Michael Joel Rosen's *Elijah's Angel* over and over!

And our kids count! Numbers are everywhere in Our Place. We count days, months, colors, shoes, pockets, loose teeth, pebbles, clouds. We measure and graph everything! Right now, our birthday graph is very popular!

We mustn't forget to tell you about the turtle. One of our colleagues from a nearby school was driving along when she saw a huge turtle in the middle of the road. Thrilled to find such a serendipitous treasure, thinking of how her second graders would love to meet such an interesting animal, she jumped out of her car to pick it up. As she carefully set it in the backseat, she remembered her school was committed to a rigid, tightly scheduled, solidly structured curriculum with little time for any diversion. Most of each day was spent preparing the children for testing, practicing skills and drills in a school-wide teaching program. Reluctantly, she gave the turtle to us.

We can't begin to describe the countless ways our turtle has inspired rich and meaningful learning experiences! Check out the shelf of books about turtles the children are reading. Their questions about turtles fill our wonder chart and have started us off on research and adventures. You'll learn from their turtle books and charts about different kinds of turtles, like snapping turtles, painted turtles, and box turtles. In the turtle log, next to the habitat they built, the children have written very interesting observations. You'll see how their handwriting is growing clearer every day. Their vocabulary continually delights us. We've discovered many turtle legends and myths from different cultures. At the beginning of the year, we didn't know that the turtle is a very important animal and symbol in many traditions! Did you? Next week at the open house, the children will present their own interpretation of the legend of Turtle Island, accompanied by original music, dialogue, chants, and dances. The costumes, props, and scenery were built from your scrounge materials. Soon you'll receive your invitation to the program, made for you by your kindergartner.

Our newest classmate, Molly, who came from China last month, is learning more and more English each day, as all her class neighbors are excellent tutors and we do so much talking all the time. (How else to learn a language but to talk a lot?) Yesterday on our field trip to a nearby field, all the children wanted to hold Molly's hand and be her helper as we celebrated our senses and wrote and drew impressions of our field study in our sketchbooks.

When you come to the open house, you'll see our classroom helpers board, with jobs for every child every day. Many of the twenty-four jobs were suggested by the kids. It takes all of us working together to contribute to the success and happiness of our group.

Included in the open-house packet you'll receive next week will be a description of developmentally appropriate practices from the National Association for the Education of Young Children, as well as an informational sheet about the multiple intelligences. (We all learn through and from our own unique mix of strengths and interests.)

We're eager to welcome you and tell you how much we love your children and how happy we are to be with them in Our Place, room 13.

> Sincerely,
> The Teachers of the Children in Room 13

P.S. We've had a few instances when children were really sick (fever, etc.) but tried to hide their symptoms so they could come to school. The third-grade brother of one of our students explained that his sister was "playing healthy" so she wouldn't miss. We were flattered but are concerned about their well-being. Thank you.

In my manic zigzags across the country to be with teachers, parents, and children, the most memorable moments are not those I spend giving keynote speeches or presenting workshops but those I spend with teachers and children, hanging out and talking off the record about what's on our minds and in our hearts. I can remember a few years ago when one of the hottest topics among teachers was *whole language.* I have heard the whole gamut of opinions and concerns, from total harmony with the gestalt philosophy of whole language to nervous questions ("Is *this* whole language? Am I doing it right?") and challenges ("I don't get it! I thought I *was* doing whole language every Thursday. Look, here are my whole-language worksheets. *What does whole language mean anyway?*").

In my more frivolous mind-sets, I have thought that the quest for the definitive explanation of whole language is like the perennial search for signs of spring. Indeed, more recently the concept of whole language has fallen out of favor in many quarters, and I think what happened is that its skeptics were trying to understand whole language just from descriptions on the printed page. If we can get beyond labels and think of the concept of whole language simply as *language in action,* language that flourishes in the rhythm of everyday life, then its signs are everywhere!

For example, one fine October day during a break in a conference in beautiful Arcata, California, Pam Goldsmith, the director of Mad River Children's Center, invited me to visit her program. I was delighted. Snooping through her cheery, colorful rooms, which were rich with developmentally appropriate materials, resources, projects, and activities, I noticed something missing.

"Pam, where are the kids?"

Mumbling "Oh-well-c'mon, we'll go see," Pam led me to the backyard. Walking out the center's back door, I couldn't help seeing the immense hole. Pam recited its measurements: eight feet wide by twenty feet long and three feet deep! From within the hole came the voices of children laughing, playing, singing, and counting. As we walked nearer, the scene grew clearer. Shoveling, probing, scooping dirt, and smoothing pathways, the children gleefully shouted as they discovered or uncovered buried toys. They hardly looked up to notice the stranger (me) standing with their director.

I forced Pam to tell me the story of this amazing hole.

"Well," she began, "one of our grandparents offered us a twenty-foot aluminum boat for the kids to play with. So we began digging a hole for the boat in our yard. Everybody—kids and teachers—brought shovels, and we dug and dug and dug for ten days!"

From the hole we could hear the children singing, "Found a pebble, found a pebble . . ." to the tune of "Found a Peanut" as they held up a newly discovered treasure.

"My pebble is a fossil!"

"I found a pirate's ring!"

The children went back to their explorations, and Pam continued the story.

"Digging the hole would have been fun just in itself! The digging would have been the end result, and everyone would have been happy. But as you see, even with the hole dug large enough for the boat, the children love nothing more than continuing to dig it and shape it and play in it."

Those first ten days of digging were joyful times, Pam reported. As the children dug, they talked about discovering buried treasures, dinosaur bones, and precious stones. They found little vials, sticks, twigs, pebbles, and miscellaneous (scrapped?) materials. They sang familiar and improvised songs. ("Found a Peanut" was their favorite.) They had counting races: Who could dig the most? the fastest? How many scoops did it take to fill the buckets? They experimented with every variety of digging arrangements: partners, small groups, and individuals. They read poems and stories about holes and dirt and dump trucks and building. Their favorite book was *Roxaboxen.*

After those ten glorious days, the hole was dug to specification. But the children found a bonus. Not only did they have a new, beautiful, huge hole, but they also had created a mountain of dirt!

"Believe it or not," Pam said, "no one cared about anything else but the hole. Every single child, everybody, all day, every day, lived in, on, and around the hole. We were thinking of changing our name to Mad River Children's Hole! Even the kindergarten kids ate snacks and lunches in the hole, on the mountain above the hole, or sitting around the hole!"

As Pam's narrative went on, the children began playing another game, "Rescue!" They slid a plank into the hole and used it as a ramp, driving their toy cars, trucks, and buses up and down it.

"Good thing you're helping . . ."

"It's a avalanche! Send a truck!"

"Help is coming. Here I come!"

As the rescue operation proceeded with admirable efficiency and cooperation, Pam talked about the rain.

"Well, later the rains came, and water collected in the hole. One day we came to school and saw that the water had frozen in the bottom."

Pam invited the kids to check it out.

She broke off a chunk of ice so the children could see it was solid. They examined the ice and dropped toys, rocks, branches, and boxes into the hole to see which objects were heavy enough to break the ice and which skidded across it. During the following days, they watched the frozen water melt, making continuous observations, such as "Last night it wasn't as cold as before" and "It got warm out, and the big piece of ice got smaller."

When the bottom of the hole was filled with mud, the hole became a dinosaur tar pit, the floor of the sea, and mud-sliding hills. The kids rolled all the tricycles (about eight) down into the hole. They had to really work to-gether to get them all out, cleaned up, and back in their places before the end of the day. The project called for responsibility, hard work, and cooperation. Problem solving became an everyday, all-the-time activity. The day the tricycles were in the hole, some kids built a ramp with plywood to ease their journey up and out.

"They really got inventive!" Pam added with a twinkle of admiration.

One day one of the kids suggested, "Let's all hold hands and see if we can reach all the way around the hole." The Mad River children and teachers held hands, encircled the hole, walked together in one direction, reversed, walked-skipped-hopped the other way, and made, as Pam described, "our own little hole dance and song!"

Using pieces of plastic rain gutter, the children built bridges across the hole, pushing their toy vehicles along as they played, talked, planned, and sang. They constantly brainstormed.

"What if we moved the bridge here?"

"Try it."

"Let's build it here."

The older, after-school K–3 kids knew they were on holy ground, and they wanted in. They turned themselves into architects and designed and built little cities and towns inside the hole, using mud shapes, blocks, rocks, PVC pipes, charms, and toys. They ran and jumped around the hole, singing mountain songs, railroad songs, and traveling songs.

At one point a few parents asked whether the hole was dangerous. Carefully evaluating every hole-centered activity—and that included virtually everything the children did (under close supervision, of course)—the staff decided the most dangerous aspect was that everyone got totally muddy. The solution: extra clothing for every child and a bag each day for carrying the muddy clothes home!

The hole at Mad River Children's Center intrigued me. I wondered about it for weeks. For months. In January, almost four months after my visit to Arcata, I called Pam and asked for an update. You know, young children are supposed to have short attention spans, and heaven knows, these kids had already broken all records with their unrelenting fascination, so I expected Pam to tell me the children were on to a new interest and off the hole.

Pam cheerfully informed me, however, that "the hole is still the center of everything! We had some bad weather and spent lots of time indoors. Even when we were inside, the talk and activities were about the hole! The kids looked out the windows at the rain and wondered how deep the water was. Would the mountain wash away? Would the yard be like a beach? Would our footsteps still show? Would our village be splattered with mud? Would we find our forgotten toys buried at the bottom of the rain-soaked hole?"

The older children spent the long indoor days drawing intricate plans and maps for their cities in the hole. The younger kids drew their own versions of maps. Now the walls of the rooms were covered with the children's designs, sketches, and maps of their hole and mountain.

People say if you dig deep enough, you'll reach China. Well, the Mad River hole bored deep enough into my imagination to inspire another transcontinental phone call to Pam some weeks later.

"What's happening?"

Five months after the initial digging of the hole, a natural disaster occurred. During a California storm, a big tree fell across the yard and covered the hole. Because the region had so much storm damage, the tree people hadn't yet arrived to cut up the tree and haul it away.

"Guess what is now the center of our center?" Pam challenged. Before I could answer, she announced, "The tree!"

Pam's kids love their tree. They build on it and in it. They climb it, sketch it, and write about it in their journals, next to their hole sketches, poems, and notes. Singing it, dancing about it, they turn it into magic, into mystery, into trolls' bridges, animal shelters, homes for insects, and nests.

Pam's voice lowered as my phone bill grew. She confided, "Here's our problem. The grandpa with the boat asked Ken Freed, our assistant director, to look at the boat.

(Remember the boat from last October?) Ken loves the boat and has spent hours asking different companies to donate their services and pull it the ten miles to the center. He's organizing a Saturday for parents to volunteer to sand, paint, and ready the boat for the children. Of course, the boat has to wait for the tree to get out of the hole!"

Pam was trying to stall the boat, distract Ken. Forget the boat!

"See, when the tree is removed, the children will rediscover their hole, with all its enchantment, its exciting contents they've forgotten about. I know they'll begin again with their love affair with the hole!"

She pondered, "If the boat finally arrives and settles into the hole, we'll just have to dig another hole!"

Black Elk, the great Oglala Sioux medicine man, said, "Anywhere is the center of the world." The children at the Mad River Children's Center demonstrated for months that a simple hole in the ground can be the center of the world!

Stories and poems about holes and earth! Songs and dances! Maps, sketches, blueprints! Journal pages! Chants and plants! Brainstorming! Scientific observations! Wonderment and explorations! Conversations and cooperation! Connections! Imaginative play! Hands-on, interactive, multilayered, direct experiences! Projects and programs! Questions and problem solving! Counting and measuring! Geology, archaeology, physics! Predictions, comparisons, and conclusions! Physical fitness!

Pam's provocative words still ring in my ears: "If everything had gone in logical, predictable [boring?]

sequence, imagine the immense learning that would have been missed."

I offer the hole in the backyard at Mad River Children's Center in Arcata, California, as a wholly delightful, holistic, wholesome example of whole language in action. Can you dig it?

Justin Coleman

Mimi Chenfeld came to our school today.
She told us all about Indians. We danced and
had lots of fun. We learned about tribes and
rain dances. I had fun. And every one had fun
all together. P.S. she got pretty carried away.

The kids in Carol and Linda's room are fascinated with knights, dragons, and castles. Today they build a castle out of blocks and scrounge materials.

"It won't be like a sand castle," one of the builders explains. "Tomorrow it will still be here!"

These prekindergarten children come from a variety of cultures, races, and religions. The animals in their room are a diverse family of classroom pets, from geckos, turtles, frogs, and fish to hedgehogs, chinchillas, snakes, and lovebirds (to name only a few). In Carol and Linda's room, the animals and children have a yearlong love affair.

The children meet in a brightly colored, improvised basement classroom (the building was not prepared for the overflow of infants, toddlers, and young children) that features numerous projects, excellent children's books, "our own art gallery," mobiles, sculptures, birds' nests, and well-used art supplies.

Almost-five-year-old Carly proudly shows me her *Carly's Book of Beautiful Planting*.

Nature, the environment, animals, seasons, and community events are some of the major areas of interest and activity. Music, dancing, reading, playing, building, painting, observing and caring for animals, experimenting, and discovering are basic ingredients in the rich mix of magical moments that define daily life in this exciting place.

Children don't walk reluctantly or hesitantly to Carol and Linda's room. *They run!* They can't wait for the day to begin, for the adventure of the day! Each morning they know they will be greeted by loving and enthusiastic teachers. They know their castle will be waiting for them. Water won't wash it away.

A few miles away at a nearby school, all the kindergarten classes and one kindergarten–first-grade combination class have caught the contagious theme of—what else?—dinosaurs. Because this school offers a program of informal education enriched by a valued arts team that works in close collaboration with the classroom teachers, each kindergarten class designs its own unique medley of explorations and information gathering. Few worksheets or workbooks in this school!

In the warm climate of continuous sharing, first-grader Karl brings in his favorite book, *The Dinosaur Stomp*. Everyone loves its wacky story about dinosaurs getting ready for their big dance, called a stomp! When Karl carries the book into Marlene's dance class, she catches the children's enjoyment and runs with it. After all, the dinosaurs are getting ready to party! Expanding on the story, the children and Marlene learn dances from around the world. Multiplying ideas, working cooperatively, and making decisions, the children combine their own movement patterns with the story of dinosaurs, with dinosaurs' time lines through history, with their stomp party! Soon *all* the kindergarten classes are in on the fun and busy planning their sharing for families and community. The kids are so excited that many of them even teach their families the dances!

The children are afraid to get sick! How could they miss even a single day? On the evening of the sharing, the children and their families don't walk to school. They stomp! They dance! They *run* to school!

Don't take my word for it. Observe young children on their way to school, to child care programs, to home care. Their feet barely touch the ground as they bound eagerly through the open doors. They can't wait to start the day. Even if they feel under the weather—sniffly, tummy-achy, itchy—they insist on not missing! The climate of their programs and the teachers in their programs, in their schools, have healing powers.

No matter what the building's structure or the age of its materials, these special places are filled with love, welcome, surprises, laughter, interesting and inviting experiences, and activities that promise challenge, delight, and success. The children know they will be safe at any speed.

Intensive themes, such as the dinosaurs I have described, are not necessary for capturing the spirit of children. Sometimes the simplest things are the best. A teacher paints a large ice cream container, cuts a small hole in it, and turns it into a mouse house. Every day, she reaches into the mouse house and finds—*ta da!*—a few letters from the mouse to different children.

Early one still-dark morning, a family hears sounds downstairs. Nervously, the parents tiptoe down, expecting to confront an intruder, only to find their kindergartner dressed and ready for school—two hours early!

"What are you doing up so soon?" the parents ask, astonished.

"I've got to get to school early today!" The child jumps with impatience. "I think I have a letter from the mouse!"

Is today the day the children will wrap bean seeds in moist paper towels, place them in plastic sandwich bags, and tuck them cozily into their pockets to make pocket gardens? Or is today the day they will watch as their bean seeds sprout before their very own eyes?

Is today the day when they will make drums out of coffee cans and cereal containers, or is today the day when their puppets will tell a story?

You can bet that in classes like these, young children are learning in enriching, multidimensional, joyful, playful, open-ended ways. Their days are rich with interesting, diverse materials and a wide variety of experiences that help them connect, find meaning, and make sense of the world.

But there is a flip side. Nowadays, with such an emphasis on academic achievement, on skills and drills and tests and benchmarks, the pressure is on to take the fun out of fundamentals.

When we round up and remove the fun, the adventures, the surprises, the celebrations of ideas, and the open-ended, active, and interactive components of the joy of learning from our children's daily experiences, we'll see more kids walking rather than running to school.

No question about it: as a major national issue, early childhood education is it. Researchers add information on a regular basis. Educators and parents, politicians and community leaders churn with dialogue and debate as they try to decide what and how young children should learn. Which way will we go with early childhood education? Will we enhance children's lives or diminish them? Will we entice the children, invite them, delight them with exciting, inspiring, memorable learning moments, hours, days? Or will we discourage and bore them? These are crucial decisions.

While the debates intensify and are all too often polarizing and political, the children have their own agendas, their own expectations. Kids tell us and show us how they want to be taught. Are we listening? Fortunately, a lot of us are listening, and a lot of kids will still be running to school!

When this was written, Carol Highfield and Linda Muzzo taught prekindergarten at the Leo Yassenoff Jewish Center's Early Childhood Program in Columbus, Ohio.

Marlene Robbins taught dance; Karen Mughan, Emilie Pitzer, Shelly Reed, and Michelle Devoll taught kindergarten; Sharon Sazdanoff taught music; Jim McMahon taught art; and Tracy McCarty taught a kindergarten-through-first-grade combination class at Indianola Alternative Elementary School in Columbus, Ohio.

"My Loose Is Tooth!"
Kidding Around with the Kids

The old folktale goes something like this: At the beginning of time, the Creator was giving out special gifts to each animal. After all the animals received their special gifts, the Creator realized that he'd forgotten to give something to the human beings. To make up for this oversight, people received the best gift of all—a sense of humor!

Meet Steve Wilson, a clinical and consulting psychologist who calls himself the World's One and Only Joyologist. His favorite motto is "If It's Not Fun, I Don't Want to Do It."

Steve easily spouts statistics and research that overwhelmingly support the importance of humor and playfulness in the classroom. He tells us that teachers who encourage laughter in their classes have children who learn more quickly, retain more, and have fewer classroom problems. He urges us to see true, healthful humor as a cathartic activity and a way of relaxing, communicating, sharing experiences, keeping brain cells open and charged, learning, comprehending, developing language, and even clarifying values.

But we work with young children! We *know* how easily and enthusiastically they laugh. Their mirth is natural. If they don't "get it," they don't force laughs to be polite. We really don't need Steve's research reports to demonstrate that children's laughter indicates comprehension, imagination, and perception. Because their language is new, young children are constantly experimenting with words and sounds and phrases, often coming up with completely original discoveries that astonish and delight.

Because our young children have not solidified stereotyped attitudes, their reactions are honest—often expressing powerful insights described in sometimes hilarious terminology.

Asked how she liked her one-year-old brother, Max, seven-year-old Saroj thought for a moment and then answered, "Forty percent."

With a group of kindergartners I was reviewing ideas from *The Wizard of Oz,* which most of the children had seen on TV that week. I wanted to close in on the tornado as an event to dance about, so I invited the class to think about the tornado as "something that comes at the beginning of the story."

Josh corrected, "It didn't come at the beginning."

"Well, close to the beginning. Early in the story," I continued.

"No," he persisted. "Not at the beginning. The tornado didn't come at the very very very beginning."

I surrendered. "Okay. Okay. So, what *did* come at the very, very beginning of the story?"

"The credits!" he announced.

Most young children have amazing memories and are very loyal to sequential events. Give them time and opportunities to share the way they see things. Not only will you learn a lot about the level of knowledge unique to each child, but you will also have many opportunities to laugh together.

Children's explanations of everyday phenomena are often highly original. They help us see connections and relationships that are surprising and refreshing and that have their own inner logic. Their laughter is frequently the laughter of surprise and discovery.

We were talking about whistling.

Six-year-old Alicia whispered to me, "Mimi, I'm a very good whistler."

I murmured a response.

"Do you know why I'm such a good whistler?" she asked.

"Why?"

"Because I have a bird."

The more I thought about her explanation, the more it soared in my mind. Of course, the hugs and loving laughter that followed warmed both of us.

Laughter is never to make fun of others. To delight with and share and celebrate together—yes. To ridicule— no. The difference makes all the difference.

Back to *The Wizard of Oz.* Another group of children had improvised many of the characters and events in the story through music, movement, and drama. At a rest, I challenged them with the question, "What happened to the Wicked Witch of the West when water was poured on her?"

Jumping up and down, the children shouted, "She melted! She melted!" Interrupting the group response, tiny Jackie, with the widest, most amazed eyes, rushed to the center and proclaimed in amazement, "Mimi, the Wicked Witch melted in *my Wizard of Oz* too!"

It was probably the very moment in Jackie's young life when she first realized she was not at the very center of the universe, that other children shared some of her own experiences, and that they had subjects in common and could have fun together confirming their knowledge. As the new lesson hit her, Jackie "got it." She led the group in merry applause.

Young children have a logic unique and pure. For example, the subject was transportation, and the kindergartners and I were gathering suggestions on various means of transportation as material for a dance. During a pause in the group's think-tank efforts, I asked, "Does anyone have any more ideas on different kinds of transportation?"

Peter immediately contributed, "Yes, Dad's shoulders!" In countless delightful ways, young children remind us of things we have forgotten. They keep telling us never to take anything for granted. They continuously make connections, even if how they express those connections is determined by the language they hear in their unique environments.

The story we were improvising had many animals in it. During a rest break, I asked the children to think of any animals we might have left out of the story. Four-year-old Timmy immediately suggested that we'd left out "chick-munks!" *Chipmunks* has never sounded right to me since.

I could share many more examples like this to remind those of us who celebrate mirth in the classroom (let every day be a "mirth" day!) of the delightful surprises in store for us. Children's natural humor comes through their interpretations of language, their honest reactions to situations and relationships, their comprehension of ideas, and their original expressions of wonder and curiosity, and it provides daily nourishment of laughter, playfulness, and imagination.

Very little is asked of the adults in the children's lives except to provide numerous opportunities for language interaction and free play and to have the good sense to appreciate the children's contributions.

But here's the *real* challenge: We must become more active participants in the humor process! We must free ourselves so we can enjoy a new way (or is it an old way?) of *being with* our students. We can be experimental, light-hearted, fun loving, and reassuring. As we help children expand comprehension, build confidence, and enjoy the learning process, we can be role models, inspirations to our children as we demonstrate through our own behavior and freedom of speech how to minimize tensions with a joke and how to loosen uptight, closed-in thinking systems with good-natured kidding.

When we take a more active part in the process, we give ourselves permission to fool around. Try "forgetting" facts. Mixing up information that children already know is guaranteed to foster good-humored fun and high-powered clarification and comprehension. And they sure do feel smart!

I always kid the children in some of these ways:

"Let's see, folks, today we're going to review one of our very favorite stories—'Goldilocks and the Seven Pigs.'"

Here are listening skills at work. *"What? 'Goldilocks and the Seven Pigs'? You mean—"* the children shout.

I interrupt their protests with a twinkly eyed apology. "Sorry about that, friends. What I mean, let's see, today we're going to review one of our very favorite stories—'Goldilocks and the Three Blind Billy Goats!'"

The variations on this theme are as numerous as ears on potatoes or eyes on corn. I mean, well, you get the idea!

Carrying the fun of mix-up a bit further, I remember the day the children and I celebrated a new turtle puppet I'd received as a gift. We improvised a version of the fable "The Tortoise and the Hare." We *all* danced the slow, determined, disciplined tortoise and the fast, jumpy, hoppy, smug hare.

When we danced the hare, we were so far ahead in the race against the tortoise that we stretched, looked for delicious carrots, and rested.

As we sat down, munching our invisible carrots, I kiddingly said, "The carrots sat under a tree eating their rabbits." The children rolled over laughing. That line became part of the story, repeated over and over with accompanying giggles each and every time.

When the tortoise won the race, I offered a play on words. "And the turtle wins by a hair!"

One of the children mischievously added, "The hairy turtle wins by a hair!"

And we ended with, "The hare lost!"

When we give ourselves permission to enjoy the playfulness of the creative process, mixing and matching and mismatching, arranging and rearranging material, we model healthy delight in ideas and relationships. When humor is shared, people feel close to and warm with each other. Cohesiveness is strengthened.

Emergency shots of humor can relieve tense situations. Minimize anxiety with laughter.

I celebrated a variation of the "Gifts of the Animals" story with yet another group. We danced all the animals as they rejoiced in their "gifts." The horses galloped. The birds flew. Kangaroos jumped.

With each new gift, we chorused, "The horses got a gallop. The birds got wings to fly with. Kangaroos got jumping feet." As the story continued, we added to the chant.

In the middle of the drama, I accidentally bumped Avi on the head with my tambourine. His face changed from sunshine to storm clouds. Tears in his eyes, lips trembly, he stopped the action. Realizing he wasn't physically hurt, I patted him and said, "And Avi got a tambourine on his head." Avi fell to the floor laughing. The other children joined him in gales of laughter.

Thus the story developed: "The horses got gallops. The birds got wings to fly with. Kangaroos got jumping feet. Avi got a tambourine on his head. Fish got fins to swim with. Monkeys got tricks. Turtles got shells."

And which part of the story did the children most enjoy? The part that turned Avi's lips from a pout to a grin: "And Avi got a tambourine on his head!"

It's never too late to begin to appreciate and use this very special gift of ours, humor. Remember, we get better at whatever we practice, so begin practicing now to enjoy and encourage the humor within and around you.

Talk with your children and listen to them. When your daily plan makes room for laughter, you'll find yourself and your children learning successfully together in loving ways. Cherish that gift!

Shiggy started it all when he wore his new firefighter's hat to our first movement session way back in September. He and his toddler colleagues came zooming into the dance room all fired up about fires. It was such a hot subject! How could I fight such enthusiasm?

Scrapping my plan to celebrate the folk tune "Old MacDonald Had a Farm" with music, dance, improvisation, animal dialogue, humor, and drama, I switched to a teacher's version of automatic pilot (in other words, I winged it) and created a story about firefighters.

"Once upon a time, the firefighters were sleeping in the firehouse." (The children dropped to the floor, closed their eyes, and snored. Debbie, their good-sport teacher, tiptoed to the corner of the room. At my signal, she burst into arm-waving, finger-vibrating, torso-swaying flames. I sounded the alarm.)

"The firefighters jumped up, dressed quickly, slid down the pole, and hurried to their fire trucks!" (The children accompanied the narrative with rapidly changing movement patterns, demonstrating dressing, sliding, rushing.)

"Sirens blaring, the fire trucks raced around the city to the fire." (We always practice moving around the room in the same direction. This safety habit is deeply instilled in all the children of our school. On this day, the fire trucks raced around the city to the bouncy beats of exciting Israeli/Arab music. Because we always have the music of the world at our fingertips, we play the music of the world with all ideas.)

"The firefighters arrived at the fire. They *uncurled* their hoses, *stretched* their ladders, *climbed up,* and *balanced* themselves as they aimed their heavy power hoses toward the flames. Finally, the fire was out!" (The fiery Debbie slowly drooped to the floor. High fives! Good job! To the percussive rhythms of African drums and bells, the fire engines raced back to the firehouse.)

Before I could steer us on to Old MacDonald's farm, as I had planned, the children sang out, "Can we do that again? Can we have another fire?" (Confession: I am a person who lets kids boss her around—especially when they are totally enthralled with an idea. I call the ideas children are madly in love with *magic vocabulary.* Obviously, "fire" headed Shiggy's classmates' magic vocabulary list.)

That day back in September, we extinguished three major fires. One of them happened on Old MacDonald's farm! Debbie got triple-aerobics points as she flared and flamed in different locations around the room.

"Is this in my job description?" she joked. "I'm almost burned-out!"

From that day on, Shiggy and his classmates rushed into every movement session with their zealous chant, "Can we do the fire story?"

I never, ever mentioned the word *fire*. Yet the fire-fighters' story was always requested by the children in Shiggy's class. Whoever said young children have short attention spans needs to visit a group of young children when they're immersed in a fascinating subject.

Confronted by this weekly challenge, I realized my choices were limited to three:

1. Burn all my plans and curriculum guides.
2. Sweetly say, "Enough is enough already with the fires! We need to get on with our other very important work!"
3. Be creative, be imaginative, be flexible, be open-minded, be playful, be holistic, be courageous, be tuned-in to the kids, and be brilliant, and figure out ways to link a fire to every other subject or topic. In other words, make connections!

Naturally, I chose number three, over and over again. Now it's months later, and I can report that Shiggy's class has not missed a chance to work with a fire story. We've integrated fires and firefighters in every session. We've put out fires:

* on Old MacDonald's farm;
* on the Yellow Brick Road (didn't poor Scarecrow almost catch fire?);
* at the circus (all those torches and fireworks);
* on the property of the Three Pigs (remember when the wolf slid down the chimney into a pot of boiling water and burned his tush?);
* in the rain forest (forest fires are very dangerous);
* on the road with Jack Be Nimble (better jump very high over that candlestick, Jack!).

Have I made the point, or are more examples necessary?

Despite all their textbooks and notebooks packed with information, despite the research and scholarship available to them, teachers and education students are always astonished at the daily situations their courses of study didn't cover—situations that demand a combination of spontaneity, flexibility, imagination, boldness, instinct, faith, playfulness, and pure nerve to guarantee intelligent and loving responses.

I am relentless when presenting the alternatives: "You're either open or closed! You're either flexible or uptight! You're either integrated or compartmentalized! Which side are you on?"

Over the last five decades, I have experienced hundreds of incidents in which super-structured, inflexible teachers slammed shut doors that would have led to opportunities for joyful learning. They have said:

"It's not in my lesson plan."
"I didn't have enough advance notice."
"It doesn't fit into our schedule."
"It's not included in our curriculum."
"We've already finished fires."

But education is a dynamic, exciting, elusive, and mysterious process. Aren't the moments we remember most clearly precisely the ones that simply *happened,* as Shiggy's firefighter story did?

Fire hats off to those creative teachers who put a marker in their daily plan books and embark with their children on adventures into uncharted territories! They design new combinations, discover amazing connections. The powerful elements of surprise, delight, appreciation, and comprehension dazzle the participants.

To such experiences we bring everything that is in us as teachers—and more. (Do we really know *all* of our gifts and resources?) The children contribute their best energy and ideas. Language flows and grows in these shared times when we are learning together on the journey.

February was a weird month. The temperature rose into the forties and fifties, ruining the kindergarten teacher's plan (marked "snow and snow people" in bold print in her calendar). She always saved "snow" for what was usually the coldest month. Her worksheets, activities, and projects were based on bundling up the children and playing out in the snow.

She could have been the kind of teacher who was rigid even when the month of February was not frigid!

But she wasn't. She could have said, "These are my well-prepared, carefully thought-out plans. Even though the air is warm and there is no snow on the ground, we are going to follow these activities to the letter! They were good enough for the last ten Februaries, and they will be good enough for now. Business as usual!"

But she didn't. Instead, with a twinkle in her eye and a hang-loose sense of humor, she shared a new idea with her kindergartners. "How about if we put bikinis on our 'snow' people?"

Giggling and using their imaginations, the children celebrated snow with figures and games. They listened to their teacher explain, "Boys and girls, if this were a regular, old-fashioned February, we would be surrounded by snow. Let's talk about snow!" And they did. They talked about weather records and statistics and average temperatures. They discussed weather patterns, made comparisons, and analyzed expectations. They learned about graphs and weather reports and predictions.

The children enjoyed the planned activities and the fun-filled changes that enriched their awareness of how unusual the weather of this particular month was. Their playful pictures expressed the new combinations.

Serendipity plays a huge part in the creative process. How do we seize the unexpected opportunities presented to us? Teachers who do not teach in the key of life have told me, "Oh, we didn't watch the convention on TV because we had already finished government."

"We don't need to look for comets because we're not up to our space unit yet."

"When Sean brought in the small totem his grand-mother carried for him from Alaska, I told him he had to wait his turn for show-and-tell. And he wasn't scheduled for another week. Besides, we don't really study Alaska this year."

At an in-service workshop I presented, "Teaching in the Key of Life," many beginning and experienced teachers expressed concern about handling spontaneous, serendipitous challenges. (It's easier to simply dismiss the opportunities presented!) I made up a story about a circus animal handler walking an elephant into a nearby elementary school. The two stood in the doorway of a classroom, waiting for the teacher to invite them in.

"Pardon me," the teacher told the animal handler politely. "Could you please get the elephant out of my room? We're finished with the letter E!"

From A to Z, we brainstormed ways to welcome the elephant!

Uh-oh, here comes Shiggy's class! Today's plan is to have a big Presidents' Day celebration. No doubt the fire department will lend us a few fire engines and firefighters to lead the festivities. What's a parade without a fleet of fire trucks? We never know when that fire alarm will go off, do we?

Dear Ms. Chenfield,
    We thank you for
coming to our school and
for teaching us the dances
to the Winne the Pooh animals.
It must be hard to learn
the dances to the Pooh animals.
You made me tired and a
lot of others. You must
get tired sometimes in your
career.

                    Your friend,
                    Benji Frank

Rain falls. Sun shines. Planets revolve. Earth turns. Fires burn. Volcanoes erupt. Gingerbread men run. Flowers grow. Clowns juggle. Frogs jump. Monkeys swing. Conestoga wagons roll. Flags unfurl. Ships sail. Archaeologists dig. Wind blows. Continents shift. Peacocks strut. Tornadoes spin. Dorothy skips.

Thank you, Howard Gardner, for legitimizing movement, music, dance, drama, and play as basic ways of learning in your wonderful multiple intelligences theory, which is now accepted by educators and philosophers the world over. We who work and play with children day by day and year by year have known forever that for so many people, the most effective ways to learn, comprehend, absorb, *know* is through movement, music, and kinesthetic experiences. Research supports the value of diverse learning methods. We are talking about making connections. It's all about helping children (and ourselves) see relationships. Learning isolated skills and facts in static settings is bad for our health!

The arts help us make the world whole. The arts are our oldest way of learning, expressing ourselves, and communicating. Our ancestors painted masterful pictures on cave walls and crafted amulets, tools, and musical instruments preserved now in the stones of ancient caves. Their paintings tell their stories. Animals were prominent subjects, but look carefully and you will see dancers and ceremonies and people caught in action. In many tribal cultures, there is no word for art. The arts are part of everything! Seasons, events, places, life passages, community traditions—the arts are the core way people honor important ideas and happenings. Children learn their culture through the arts.

No matter what grade, age, or subject you teach, think *connections.* Draw a circle. In the center of the circle, in the hub, draw the children and the idea you want to convey. Draw many spokes (different spokes for different folks!). Write *dance, music, story, drama, poetry,* and *visual arts* on the spokes. Don't leave out the standard curriculum areas, such as reading, math, and social studies. All will connect to the central idea, to the children learning in their best, most successful combination of ways. And remember, movement, dance, and music are very old ways. If your environment is one of trust and love, the words *show me* will be magical words that inspire children to respond with bodies in shapes and motion.

During the fifty years I've been bouncing around the education field, we've danced and moved to depict people escaping slavery and finding safety stations on their way to freedom; the galloping chariot of Apollo carrying the sun across the sky; all the king's horses racing to help Humpty Dumpty; the transformations of caterpillar to butterfly, tadpole to frog; the heaviness of molecules in cold fronts; the dynamic pageant of moving seasons; the wheels of the bus on the way to the zoo; number facts and spelling words; and the parts of speech and famous speeches.

Every idea is a universe of possibilities. Every idea, lesson, and concept can be enriched by movement, by dance. Connecting movement to all areas of the curriculum, to all skills, is natural. The arts are the connective tissue that holds our spirits intact. Without the arts as part of our lives, we would be truly handicapped.

As we believe, so we teach. If we believe music, dance, poetry, chant, mime, visual arts, and drama are separate and sometimes unequal human activities having little relationship to anything else, that's the narrow message we'll transmit to our children.

If we believe all concepts, topics, and themes have countless built-in dimensions of learning, we will help our children make discoveries, delight in surprise, and celebrate comprehension as they grow in awareness, knowledge, and skills.

All of our children are waiting, are eager to be invited to ways of learning that are joyful, meaningful, relevant, and multilayered.

On the way home from his preschool program,

two-and-a-half-year-old Micah told his mommy about his morning.

She asked him, "How was movement with Mim?"

He said, "I helped Mim today."

"How?" asked Mom.

"I jumped!"

The children will help us remember what we know but sometimes forget: education is a moving experience! Get moving!

Can a Fish Snap Its Fingers?

"Can a frog clap its hands?"

we ask, clapping.

"*No!*" The three-year-olds shake their heads as they clap.

"Can a caterpillar clap its hands?"

"*No!*" they chorus.

"But *we* can!" And we do.

"Now we stamp our feet. It's fun to stamp feet. Softly, forcefully! Tiptoe, march! Imagine—we can stamp our feet! Can a duck stamp its feet?"

. "*No!*" The children stamp.

"Can a mosquito stamp its feet?"

"*No!*"

"But isn't it something? *We* can!" And we do.

"Let's snap fingers. Sometimes it's hard for small children to snap fingers. Tickle the air. Brush your thumb.

There you go! Snapping fingers is great! Can an elephant snap its fingers?"

"*No!*" *Snap. Snap. Snap.*

"Can a kangaroo snap its fingers?"

"*No!*"

"Can a fish snap its fingers?"

"My fish can!" one little boy announces proudly.

We begin with the wonder of it. Whether we're a class of three-year-olds, junior-high wisecrackers, or forgotten residents in homes for the aged, we begin with the wonder of it—that we can move.

In classrooms, gyms, all-purpose rooms, basements, and recreation rooms, in homes for the aged, meeting rooms in community centers, hospital wards, and church and synagogue halls, we have moved with fellow humans from 2 to 102.

Ideas for moving are infinite. We have scrapped careful plans in order to use an "idea of the moment" contributed by an eager child in spontaneous conversation. We have even changed lessons for birthdays.

"Dotty is five today." Dotty proudly smiles. "Well, folks, we have to do something special for a birthday, don't we?" And we junk our scribbled notes for the day. "How many other five-year-olds are there?" Half the class raises hands. "How many are going to be five?" The other half responds. "Five is a super-good number. Let's do everything in fives for our birthday child. What can we do in fives?"

"We can jump five times!" Sandy says. We jump five times. We run five times. We skip five times. We hop on one foot five times. We spend our session rolling, crawling, leaping, sliding, marching, twirling, spinning, bending, stretching, wiggling, flying, somersaulting—*five times.* Dotty leaves glowing. She is thoroughly, deeply five now. In all her limbs and muscles.

Ideas. Ideas. They don't have to be complicated. You don't need a doctorate in dance to enjoy a simple movement.

"How many ways can we go from this end of the room to the other? I bet we can find twenty-five ways!"

The class doubts.

"What's one way we can cross the room?"

"Walk."

"Right on! Let's walk."

"What next?"

"Skip."

"Good for you! Okay, let's skip. That's two ways. Twenty-three more to go!"

The children think of twenty-five ways easily. The class is over, and tired children are still throwing out suggestions like confetti.

"Skip backwards?"

"Slide?"

"We can think of fifty ways easily, can't we, Mimi?"

We dance every animal. Children love animals. They hop like rabbits, roar and run like lions, stumble like new deer, gallop like horses.

We talk about caterpillars turning into butterflies. I share my son's long-ago question, "Do caterpillars *know* they're going to turn into butterflies?" The children drift with the thought. We imagine how it would be to be a caterpillar who mysteriously and magically and scientifically becomes a new creature. We feel it in our bodies. We sleep in our dark cocoons, curl into ourselves. Great silence is the music of the room. Silence and metamorphosis. A soft drumbeat begins our change. Beautiful butterflies of every color and size emerge. Even the roughest boys sprout wings and float gently. The room brightens.

"When I see a butterfly next summer," Debby whispers, "I'll know just how it feels."

"'Christopher Robin goes / Hoppity, hoppity, / Hoppity, hoppity, hop. . . .'" We singsong the poem. The children do not need to be told. They hop. And hop. And hop. "'Whenever I tell him / Politely to stop it, he / Says he can't possibly stop.'"

We move from being the smallest dots imaginable to the hugest giants. We bounce like balls and turn into elves, witches, and fierce kings; bears searching for honey and escaping from bees; chicks cracking through shells; skaters skidding; basketball players dribbling; circus clowns tumbling; acrobats balancing; and snow shapes melting.

We stay very still. Now move just one part. Move another part. And another. The miracle of the moving parts. Now move two parts of you. Another two. Now three—four—five!

We make Thumbelinas with our thumbs and watch them dance. We dance like all the toys in the toy store: windup toys that spring to action, then slow down; cars, trucks, trains, planes; limp rag dolls that leap into limp rag-doll dances; and fluffy soft toys that make everyone feel wonderful.

We imagine the sounds our bodies would make as they move. We make the sounds of a finger wiggling, a head shaking, feet kicking, a back bending, arms waving. We wear a happy-face button and wonder how we would move if we were happy faces. How would a happy face move shoulders? Arms? Heads? Feet? How would a happy face dance?

With older boys and girls, we play with challenges. Go from up to down in chunks, in pieces. Falling apart. Smoothly. Fiercely. Bounce down! Collapse!

Go from down to up, reaching. Grasping. Pleading. Chopping. Expanding. Untangling. Unwinding. You can do downs and ups forever and never run out of variations. Turn your body into a giggle, into a cheer. A whimper. A whisper. A scream. A warning. A moan.

Make three different body shapes for:

* Work	* Welcome	* Hello	* Play
* Good-bye	* Friend	* Help	* Enemy
* Warm	* Cold	* War	* Peace

Anyone who can move can make body shapes, body designs. Pretend you're the designer of a poster for those ideas. Work alone or in groups. Work one idea with another, and one idea against another.

Join groups together to make a machine of bodies. Each group becomes a part of the machine. The machine has moving parts. It stops and starts. Some parts go fast, some slow. Sometimes the whole machine moves from place to place.

We talk about refugees. Refugees of time. People leaving the known and familiar, leaving beloved places and things. Gathering immediate necessities and moving directionlessly to strange lands. We wonder how it feels to be lost and wandering, with no roots. We feel it in our bodies—the heaviness of it, the vagueness of it, the forlornness of that painful situation. We move with no focus, no aim. Some move alone—slowly, falteringly. Some move with others—protective, close together. Through moving we can feel.

The newspaper features a story about a Florida Native American chief who was called on to perform a rain dance after scientists had failed to end a drought. The chief danced, and lo, it did rain. We talk about ritual dances, a form of movement transcending time and cultures. Dances for good crops. Dances to ward off evil. Dances of blessing. Dances of warning. Dances of growing. Dances of healing. Everyone chooses a dance. Each child improvises. The improvised ritual dances are as effective as any witnessed on a stage. We are awed by the discovery of our own creative depths.

There's no end to ideas. Wherever you are, ideas fall around you. Pick them up. Take them. Change them. Use them. Listen to the children and listen to yourself. Movement is native to human beings.

Every teacher knows that in a classroom climate of trust and warmth, where no child is threatened and each one feels important, respected, and welcomed, joyful education is possible. Movement is a delightful experience that each may share.

This morning the sky was grim gray. Wind and rain whipped the wet streets. My car stalled and sputtered on the way to the center, where I have three classes of preschoolers and one class of adults. In each preschool class, we danced a storm. Some of us puffed up like heavy storm clouds, gathered together, and hid the sun. The sun tried to show through, but we clouds wouldn't let it. Thunder roared. Some of us moved like thunder, roaring and rolling around the room. Rain poured down. We scattered rain with our arms and fingers in a lightning jab. We jumped into the air. Wind blew. We huffed around the room, whirling and spinning. Small animals hid from the storm. Birds huddled in nests. Squirrels rushed to trees. Turtles pulled in their heads. The children were rain, clouds, lightning, thunder, birds, wind, squirrels, and turtles. One little girl lay still on the floor.

"What are you?" I whispered as storm movement raged around us.

"I'm a puddle," she replied.

The storm blew over. The group moved from one end of the room to the other. The heavy, puffed-up rain clouds softened into fluffy, floating clouds. The sun shone through. All the little animals sniffed, crawled, flew, yipped, or ran into the sunny air. Happiness beamed on every face.

This afternoon as I left the center, the clouds were breaking up. The sun burst through. Now, as I write, the sky is clear. The air is still. The colors of the day are shining.

I know the scientific explanations of storms, but I also know the magic of dance. I know in my toes that this morning, forty three-year-olds and one adult exorcised the rain from the day.

The telephone rings. The mother of one of the three-year-olds tells me, "Anthony is convinced that he caused the sun to shine today."

We begin and end with the wonder of it: that we can move!

"Wanna play?"

"Wanna play?" The most popular question of my childhood!

"Wanna play?" The most welcomed invitation of my childhood! And what did we play? Handed-down games like Jacks, Stickball, Kick-the-Can, Statues, Hide 'n Seek, Stoopball, Tag, Marbles, Hopscotch (we called it Pottsie), Toss Cards, Giant Steps, Mother May I?, One Potato, Cat's Cradle, Red Rover, Follow the Leader, Jump Rope, Allie-Allie-in-Free, bouncing ball rhymes like "A, My Name Is—."

And what else did we play? Made-up games like House, School, Hospital, Zoo, Circus, Jail, Jungle, Detectives, Restaurant, Office, Lost, Castle, Monsters, Blind, Pirates, Invisible, Movie Stars, Heidi, Peter Pan, Wizard of Oz.

And what did we play with? Marbles, tin cans, skate keys, sticks, ropes, string, chalk, stones, dolls that we named.

And what was the magic? Towels tied into capes, ribbons brightened into crowns, sheets draped over umbrellas that became tents, cigar boxes locked into treasure chests.

Contrary to popular myths that children have short attention spans, our games went on and on . . . and on. Sometimes for weeks. Sometimes for months. Sometimes a game ended only when the family moved! Deep down, I think my parents would have been reluctant to admit that this was the reason our family moved so often.

Our games taught us rules. We learned to interact in meaningful and enjoyable ways. We learned about structure.

Our games taught us different roles. Through improvisation, imitation, and invention, we tried on different possibilities. We understood more of the complex interplay between personalities and positions.

Our made-up games were exercises in positive human relations and the imagination. As we learned to speak in many voices, tackling challenging ideas and concepts, our language developed. We learned our language by *using* our language in complicated, delightful, and integrated ways.

Our games taught us skills. Our competence grew in physical, social, intellectual, and psychological areas. We manipulated and controlled our environment. We learned how things worked. We were *never* bored!

Today there seem to be a growing number of anxious parents concerned their children may be wasting precious learning time with these kinds of homemade, hand-me-down games and imaginative play. They believe policy makers who say that in this super-competitive, technological society we need to start preparing our children at very early ages for success and achievement. They believe kids need fewer playgroups and storybooks and more reading groups and workbooks.

So many teachers tell me they're getting pressured to cut back on open-ended, spontaneous free time for children in favor of formalized structures, tight-fitting programs with predetermined outcomes, constant adult intervention, and strong direction. They tell me more parents expect to see tests and scores and feel that if something isn't tested and doesn't have a grade, it doesn't count. It's a frill!

Contrary to these opinions, research clearly supports the vital importance of play in the lives of children. From the National Association for the Education of Young Children to the Association for Childhood Education International, virtually all of the professional education organizations have published major policy statements reaffirming the central role of play in child development. Books by leading scholars discuss the impact of the loss of play. The titles of two such examples indicate the strong concern: *The Disappearance of Childhood* by Neil Postman and *The Hurried Child* by David Elkind.

I am influenced by research. But I'm also affected by direct observation and experience. From my decades-old collection of countless incidents demonstrating children's love for self-directed, informal, imaginative play, I choose these three to share with you.

Ricky's parents, who are members of the New-Toy-of-the-Day Club, have turned his room into a dazzling display of flashing, computerized, stereophonic, electrical recreation equipment. On the day of our visit, we find Ricky deep in concentrated play. What is he playing with? His new video game? His set of television cartoon-inspired Transformer characters? His power-driven space station? None of the above. Ricky, head bent forward with intense focus, is playing with his three favorite toys: a cardboard paper towel roll, a cardboard box, and flexible, bendable straws!

Peter flies into preschool, a towel wrapped around his shoulders.

"Hi, Pete," I greet him.

"I'm not Pete," he informs me.

"Who are you?"

"Superman!"

"Well, Superman, we're delighted to have you with us today."

Superman flies through our warm-up exercises, zooming across the bridge as we dramatize the "Three Billy Goats Gruff," flashing his cape as he frightens off the troll.

As we say good-bye at the end of the session, I hug him and wave. "Bye, Superman."

"I'm not Superman," he informs me.

Uh-oh, I think to myself. He's probably already changed back to his regular Peter self. "Who are you?" I ask.

"Clark."

Chad, almost four years old, is playing in his front yard with his sitter, Louise, who is watching him nearby. Talking to himself, lost in his story, transfixed in a private segment of his drama, Chad suddenly spurts into action, jumping high into the air. His jump startles Louise, who runs to him anxiously.

"Are you okay? Be careful!"

Chad looks at her, bewildered. What's her problem? he wonders.

"Maybe you've had enough outside play, honey," Louise worries. "How about going in and watching your TV program."

Chad looks up at her and advises, "Chill out, Louise."

What lesson do these experiences teach us? Never underestimate a child's fascination with make-believe. In my years of teaching, I've amassed a storehouse of children's observations, evaluations, and blunt comments. The most memorable came from a child who tugged at her mother's sleeve as I, a Bronx-born, middle-aged Jewish American, came toward them on a Columbus,

Ohio, street. Pointing at me, the child said, "Mommy, that old Indian came to our school!"

The best of the evaluations came from a group of kindergartners who after our session together told their teacher, "That Mimi is a very playful girl!"

This "old Indian" would like to quote almost-four-year-old Chad and urge our anxious American families, intent on pushing and pressuring and lobbying children and their teachers, to "chill out, Louise!"

This "playful girl" prays that one day all our children will look back and cherish the memory of an invitation— an invitation to engage in hours of delight, discovery, shared learning, language expansion, and positive human relations, an invitation to gymnastics for the imagination—"Wanna play?"

We Drew a Circle That Took Him In

Randy is in your class. See him,
with the half-closed eyes and slumpy back, leaning against
the wall when everyone else is jumping with the excitement of an idea? Why is his head on the table while other
eyes are beaming their brights on you? Randy doesn't
respond when you ask a question or seem to be listening
when you read a story. *What to do about Randy?*

Through all these long school years, through all the
Randys, I've agonized over these questions: Where do we
go wrong? How can we reach these children? What can
we do to connect with them? The Randys whose behavior was labeled "disturbed" in addition to "tuned out"
or "turned off" were referred to trained psychologists or
counselors. The majority of the Randys, however, weren't
seen as needing professional treatment. Their teachers
viewed them as simply indifferent or nonparticipating.

Through all these long school years, through all these Randys, I've threatened, pleaded, bribed, nudged, cajoled, whimpered, and begged. None of my approaches succeeded in changing catatonic-looking Randys into healthy, involved, active children. But as many of us do, I adhered to that age-old practice: if it doesn't work, keep doing it! For years, I kept doing it and it didn't work, so finally I decided to look at the Randys from a different perspective. I changed my head! I turned on my windshield wipers. I cleared my vision.

It was the experience of my friend Candace Mazur, who works with the Greater Columbus Arts Council's Artists-in-Schools program, that reminded me of something I already knew but had forgotten. One day she saw a nonparticipating Randy standing apart, semiwatching her imaginative troll celebrations with a large group of children. She glanced at that Randy but had no time to do anything special to catch him in her web of enchantment. She thought to herself, Can't win them all, and turned her attention back to the group.

That night at the school's open house, a couple came toward her, gushing with enthusiasm. "Whatever you did today, Candace, you really turned our son on! Why, that boy came home from school, ran to his room, and changed it into a troll's den!"

You guessed it. The couple were Randy's parents! Over the years I'd forgotten that most of the nonparticipating Randys, half-listening, their flags at half-mast, are really with us. They go home and report on "what we did today." In many cases, parents never know their child hasn't demonstrated one gesture of interest inside the classroom.

Contributing to my new insight now is a strong new approach. It's based on the following beliefs, and it works!

> *There is no way any child can be left out of anything we do!*

> *There is no way any child can leave himself or herself out of anything we do!*

Even if our Randys are as frozen as a lava-stone Pompeii figure or as turned off as a power failure, to my way of thinking, these children are with us. Our circle takes them in. Here's some of the vocabulary that reflects this *way* of teaching—that is, teaching in the key of life:

"We need someone to watch the parade. Thanks, Randy."

"Oh, who will be the audience for our circus? Randy, thanks for volunteering!"

"We need someone waiting for the group to come home from the zoo. Randy, will you be the person waiting? Thanks a lot!"

"Randy, will you be the person standing at the corner, waiting for the traffic to pass? Thanks!"

Now after a while Randy is bombarded with participation suggestions. Mind you, he hasn't moved one muscle! He hasn't even agreed to the offers. But because my blood type is "B positive," I believe he is always participating, appreciated, and needed.

Let me tell you about our latest Randy. This Randy

has not budged in my movement sessions with his kinder-garten class since September. But he's never left out. (See examples above of how he's included.) I must confess, however, that over these months I have lost it and resorted sometimes to kidding. "Randy, don't overdo it! Don't strain yourself!" Once in a while I've tricked him into a trace of a smile.

This has continued for three seasons. Now we're into spring, and today I'm waiting for Randy's class. His teacher wants us to enrich our study of nutrition. I'm ready with a curriculum.

The kindergartners bounce in. My eyes blink. Am I seeing things? Is that Randy bouncing in with the oth-ers? I'm in shock. Randy is dancing over to me. Randy is excited. Randy bursts with the news!

"Mimi! I can snap!"

Randy's hand is in the air. Randy's fingers snap, crackle, pop. Castanet fingers. Randy is proud. He can't stop snapping. This calls for immediate response. Now, a super-structured teacher might say, "That's nice, Randy. But we're not scheduled for snapping until the third week in May. Can you hold your snap?" or "Randy, this isn't sharing time. Why not wait till next Tuesday's sharing time to show us your snap," or "Snapping is interesting, Randy, but today we are studying nutrition, so snap out of it!"

But as you know, creative teachers improvise and invent a lot. Here's what happened. I said, "Randy! This is amazing! Are you a mind reader? How did you know we're doing a story today that desperately *needs* snapping?"

Randy is hopping with excitement.

Here's the story I instantly make up. We do it with movement (of course) and drama (of course) and music (of course) and language skills (of course) and follow it with pictures and words (of course).

"Those of you who can snap, get ready. Those who can't, fake it."

We snap fingers.

"Once upon a time it was raining (snap). Thundering (we boom)! Lightning (we jab)! Far from their homes, rabbits were playing. Oh, no! Rain! The rabbits hop quickly back to their rabbit hutches."

I turn on bouncy music. We all hop back to our shelter. Randy the hopping rabbit moves with his rabbit friends as if he's been moving with them since birth.

"The rabbits reach their shelter. They shake off the rain. They talk in rabbit language translated into English. What do you think they say?"

"I got rain in my ears." (Gretchen)

"My tail is all wet." (Jeremy)

"I hopped in a puddle." (Melissa)

Oooops! The teacher is glaring at me. What happened to nutrition? Not to worry!

"Well, now the rabbits are ready to sleep. What nutritious snack can they have before bedtime?"

"Carrots!" (Jordan)

"Lettuce!" (Mitchell)

You get the idea, dear reader, and so the story continued. The rain kept falling in finger snaps. The thunder and lightning kept thundering and lightning, booming and jabbing. Far from their homes, horses, birds, deer, and children galloped, flew, leaped, and jogged. Of course, when all of these animals and humans reached home and dried off, they ate nutritious snacks. What nutritious snacks can you think of?

The whole session took fifteen minutes—from the time the children came bouncing in, to Randy's snappy announcement, to the story with at least five separate chapters, to the summary of nutritious snacks.

As miraculously as a snake sheds its skin, as Leo the Late Bloomer blooms, Randy the Snapper charges into life. But because in our time together Randy has always participated ("Thanks for being the person who isn't paying attention, Randy!"), we couldn't express our monumental astonishment and joy! Because we never let his circles leave us out and always drew our circles to take him in, when he really jumped in, it was just a lovely, everyday event—no big thing.

In my notebook I scribbled, "From Catatonic to Hyperactive: Randy Snapped Today." No big thing? Then why after school that day did the kindergarten teachers and I laugh and cry?

Let's Keep the "L" Word

It's dismissal time. Marilyn Cohen, a little more dressed up than usual in preparation for an early evening school program, holds hands with her friendship circle of kindergartners as they sing their good-bye song. When the last child leaves, waving a fistful of artwork, Marilyn hurries to check the incubator, which is on a table in the center of the room. It's been the center of attention for the last month. She tidies up the poems, projects, pamphlets, and posters (the four Ps!) that are scattered around the incubator. She places two of the children's most beloved books back on the shelf: Millicent Selsam's *Egg to Chick* and Ruth Heller's *Chickens Aren't the Only Ones.*

She checks the eggs again, and then glances at the children's chick-hatching calendar, though she knows full well what it says. It says "Day 21," but not one of the eggs shows any signs of hatching.

Staring at the apparently lifeless eggs, Marilyn thinks of the weeks of effort put into this activity: observing, comparing, discussing, researching, anticipating. And all the fun: stories, songs, games, and poems the children enjoyed as they waited for the chicks to magically hatch— one, then another, and another. Child after child has asked, "They *will* hatch, won't they, Mrs. Cohen?" How can she face her students and tell them that their fears have been confirmed, that their loving care and dedication have yielded nothing, nada, zero, zilch!

Disappointment often drives teachers to leave the profession, but Marilyn doesn't give in to disappointment. She rushes to the office telephone and dials the number of Dr. Richard Langenbach. Years ago, the embryologist/farmer visited her class and conducted an in-service presentation on chick hatching. Marilyn was among those enchanted by his wisdom and enthusiasm. Since then Dr. Langenbach has supplied eggs to Marilyn and her kindergartners for their springtime chick-hatching celebration, and their success rate has been outstanding—until now. Dr. Langenbach answers the phone, and Marilyn is relieved to hear his voice.

"Do you have any chicks up your sleeve?" she jokes, and then explains her predicament. "I'm not going to lie to the children," she assures him. "Tomorrow we'll talk about nature and how sometimes things don't work out the way we plan, the way we hope. Sometimes it's not in our hands. We do our best, but then nature has its own plan. It's hard to understand, but we have to accept that. However, I do want the children to see chicks tomorrow in order to understand what theirs would have looked like if the chicks had hatched the way we hoped they would."

She arranges to borrow about half a dozen live chicks, cancels her immediate plans, and drives fifteen miles to Dr. Langenbach's farm out in the country. But he isn't there.

"He must have forgotten," says Mrs. Langenbach, explaining that her husband left just a few minutes before. Marilyn, determined not to leave empty-handed, asks if Mrs. Langenbach would round up some chicks for her.

"Oh, my! I'm allergic to all those chickens," Mrs. Langenbach says apologetically. "I never go back there! But you're welcome to if you'd like."

So Marilyn digs her high heels into the muddy earth and heads for the chicken coops. "I didn't see this in my job description," she muses. She's greeted by a cacophony from hundreds of clucking, flapping, squawking, agitated chickens.

Where are the chicks? As she searches, she recalls how Dr. Langenbach talked about the developmentally appropriate practice of integrating chicks into the adult population. She peeks into the coops, and the birds peck her and scratch her. She finds herself in a flurry of chicken-coop dust, feathers, and empty seed husks.

Amid the cackling chaos, Marilyn manages to capture six chicks. She puts the frightened little creatures into a cardboard box she'd brought, then gladly accepts Mrs. Langenbach's offer of a washing facility. She drives back to her classroom and gets the chicks settled into their temporary homes.

The next day as her students arrive, they are thrilled to see the chicks. Marilyn explains to them where the chicks came from. They all talk about life's disappointments and joys—of eggs that don't hatch and of those that do.

All the students are photographed holding a chick. The photos will always be reminders of this special time.

Some would call Marilyn's experience an example of professionalism. Others would say she's nuts. I offer it as an example of that vital ingredient in good teaching that we seem to be more nervous about saying out loud these days: The "L" word. Every day, in ways rarely noted, teachers of all subjects and grade levels, in every town and city in this country, demonstrate the meaning of love. Marilyn Cohen is just one example. Here are some more:

* Rosie postpones the surgery she needs until summer because she doesn't want to leave her third graders in the middle of the school year.
* Marcella rises at five on trash collection days and drives around the neighborhood to find discarded but perfectly good items she can use in instructional activities with her students.
* John turns down an invitation for a special breakfast program. The tall Texan explains he just can't miss his Head Start class, where he greets every child at the door with a "Howdy, pardner! I'm mighty glad to see you!"
* Maddy holds an umbrella over her toddler

construction workers for more than an hour to shade them from the hot sun while they dig tunnels and roadways in the sand to create a storybook world.

✳ Rashid waits in line at the mall for two hours to get an autograph from a visiting sports celebrity for one of his eighth graders who is a big fan.

✳ Maxine calls every one of her fifth graders' families to make sure they attend a poetry and art celebration at the local museum. She refuses to let any child miss out and spends the evening carpooling with those who have no ride.

✳ A newspaper headline reads "Teachers Buy Extras, Survey Says: More Than $400 Spent on Supplies." The article begins, "Whether for stickers, markers, a meal on a field trip, books, or even shoes, teachers say they regularly dip into their own pockets to help their students." Jeff knows all about that. He spends more than $1,000 a year on his fifth graders. He knows which ones can't afford lunch during field trips or bus fare for special outings, so he pays for them rather than see them be excluded.

In our high-tech, ever more impersonal society, where we are often known more by our numbers than our names, it's reassuring to know that those special people teaching our children demonstrate the meaning of that trite, devalued "L" word—love.

There, I said it!

Marilyn Cohen taught kindergarten for twenty-eight years at Bet Shraga Hebrew Day School in Albany, New York.

Linda O. isn't climbing the walls

today. She's climbing on her science table, reaching up to add a new number to the line of days she and her children have been counting together. The number line is hanging on the wall above her science table. Now she's ready to climb down. While her first graders watch, she puts one foot on the table and rests the other foot on the adjacent desk, which, unbeknownst to her, is set on wheels. The desk (with one of her legs precariously perched on top of it) begins to roll away from the science table (with her other leg precariously perched on it). In silent fascination, the children's eyes widen as they watch the table and desk go their separate ways. Linda O. is hanging in midair in an almost perfect split when the desk rolls totally away from the table, dumping her splat in the middle of the floor.

Although the pain is intense and she is convinced this may be her last day on earth, Linda is a professional, a veteran teacher, so instead of crying out, calling 911, weeping and flailing in raw agony, she catches her breath and softly instructs her students to "please continue tracking along the story we were reading." The first graders bend obediently to the task, averting their eyes from their fallen teacher, who is still grounded in the middle of the floor and seeing stars. The only sound in the room is the studious turning of pages.

Linda O. is sweating profusely as the pain intensifies. She still can't move. From her splattered, semi-split position on the floor, she hears the trip-trap of little footsteps. One of her first graders is walking toward her, telling her something in a lispy voice.

"Mithus O, I brought you thum tithues. I don't know why you're thweating. You're not doing anything!"

Because this happens a few weeks before Thanksgiving (and you know what a busy and exciting time that is for first graders, what with history and environment and harvest and multicultural arts activities), Linda O. doesn't want to miss a day of school. Once she gets on her feet, she continues to teach. When school is out for the holiday, she limps through the building, dragging her seriously injured leg behind her. Three weeks after her fall, she finally visits the doctor. After examining her leg and studying the X-rays, the doctor is amazed.

"Linda, you broke your leg! I have never seen anyone with a break like this still be able to get around!"

His amazement triples when he sees that her broken leg is healing itself.

Linda O. explains it this way: "He doesn't realize I'm a first-grade teacher!"

Oh, no! It's that "L" word again! You won't find many illustrations of that word in newspaper headlines or TV features. Good news doesn't have the appeal of disaster in our violence-celebrating culture. But examples of the "L" word abound in schools and classrooms throughout the country—yes, examples of that corny, overused, unde-rused, misused, unmentionable, sorely needed word in action!

I once saw a poster that said, "The Best Way to Send an Idea Is to Wrap It Up in a Person." So let's look at a few more of the people who wrap up in themselves the idea of loving and caring about our children and making a difference in their lives. Most of them don't talk about the "L" word. They just do it, live it, *are* it!

Call it professional. Call it dedicated. Call it overly committed. Call it responsible. Let's just come right out and say what it really is: Love.

While presenting at a large conference, I'm told about the teacher's aide who spends time with early childhood special-needs children and who, as a trained catheterizer, dispenses medical assistance with gentleness and caring. Voted the Outstanding Teacher's Aide in the state, he passes up the luncheon in his honor because he doesn't want the child who needs catheterization to feel uncomfortable with the stranger who would sub for him.

"First things first," he tells me.

Rose looks weird today! Why is she wearing eyeglasses mended clumsily with masking tape? Why is her hair braided into queer pigtails standing straight up in the air?

Most of the time, Rose's inner-city third graders get along just fine and feel safe in the caring environment that is their classroom. But at other times, like today, the kids can be mean. One of Ms. Stough's third graders has lice again. Everyone knows about it because her hair is swathed in petroleum jelly and tied straight up, away from her scalp, in tight pigtails. The kids have been teasing her, so Rose ties her own hair into pigtails and stands with her arm around the little girl.

This same day, a boy's eyeglasses break. Rose mends the frames with masking tape, and they look klutzy and funny. Again, the teasing; again, Ms. Stough to the rescue. She winds tape around her own unbroken glasses. The teasing stops. The message is clear.

"I get kidded and razzed by the teachers and parents," Ms. Rose admits, "but those kids are safe."

Another example of the "L" word in action comes from a letter written by Barbara Selinger about her day spent substituting in a special education class of ten children from kindergarten through second grade. The children face daily emotional, physical, and behavioral challenges. Barbara puts in an exhausting day, and in the last few minutes, she sits down with a second grader who is quietly working alone. She asks if he needs help. He nods. His assignment is to pretend it's the first day of school and to write about what he had hoped school would be like and whether it is, in fact, what he had hoped. The child has nothing to write. Barbara prods him with a few questions and receives minimal responses.

She asks him if he had hoped to meet a new friend on the first day of school, and he shrugs as he replies, "I don't have *any* friends. *Nobody* likes me and no one wants to be my friend."

Barbara says she disagrees with him, but they go on to write about a plain, ordinary day where nothing good happens. When he finishes, she asks him, "Can I tell you a secret?"

He nods.

She whispers in his ear that *today* he made a new friend.

He looks at her with big, questioning eyes.

Barbara asks, "Do you know who?"

"You?" he answers.

When Barbara says yes, the biggest grin brightens his face—a smile from ear to ear.

Barbara's letter ends with "At that moment I remembered why I became a teacher."

Admire the wall-to-wall ribbons of honor earned by boys who are court-assigned to the Riverview Juvenile Correctional Center. Troubled boys. Boys in trouble whose ages range from twelve to twenty. It's a tough place for the boys and for their teachers.

Six years ago, in spite of probably justified skepticism, science teacher Paul Robinson got an idea. Taking his students to a field outside the building, he inspired them with the possibility of planting a vegetable garden. It took hard, sweaty work to dig the new garden, but they did it. They planted many kinds of seeds—eggplant, pumpkin, squash. But the most important seeds Paul and the boys planted were seeds of confidence, self-esteem, responsibility, cooperation, community, patience, and stewardship of the earth. When Paul and the boys took their vegetables to the county fair that first year, they won top prizes and honors. Since then they have won many state and county awards. Now, with the assistance of his colleagues Jana Schelb and Dan Shealey, Paul and the boys have a colorful and bountiful garden blooming.

When I acknowledge the extra time, effort, and faith involved in this ongoing project, Paul simply says, "It makes science interesting, doesn't it?"

I wouldn't say it to this tough, dedicated educator, but I think—oh, no! It's the "L" word again!

To be continued—indefinitely.

Linda O'Brien and Rose Stough taught for many years in the Columbus, Ohio, public schools. Barbara Selinger made friends with kids in the Glen Ridge schools in Glen Ridge, New Jersey. Paul Robinson, Jana Schelb, and Dan Shealey grew prize-winning vegetables with the boys at Riverview Juvenile Correctional Center in Delaware, Ohio.

Dedicated to Sylvia Ashton-Warner's wonderful reminder that before we teach others, we must teach ourselves.

You say you're not creative!

You shrink from that "C" word. Well, I'm here to tell you that you *are* creative. Listen up!

You are a member of a very creative family. You're *not* a green bean, a lima bean, a baked bean, or a kidney bean. You're a human bean, and you have been given a gift of creativity as part of your heritage, your legacy, your designer genes!

Don't limit your interpretation of that "C" word to the making of a creative product like a poem, dance, or painting. That "C" word encompasses process as well as product. It has to do with a way of thinking, of being, of living. It's about flexibility, spontaneity, serendipity, openness, playfulness, experimentation, exploration, connections, combinations, changes, rearranging, and arranging.

Whenever you walk up to a salad bar and fill your plate with a selection of the offerings, you participate in a creative act. Think about it. Do *all* the plates held by *all* the customers look exactly the same after they are filled with salad items? *Of course not.* Each plate is an expression of a unique individual.

Visit a high-rise apartment building where each unit has exactly the same layout. Knock on every door. Even though the floor plans are identical, are all the apartments designed and decorated exactly the same? *Of course not.* Each dwelling space is an expression of a unique individual.

Check out a flower shop or greenhouse. Note the contents of passing shopping carts. Each reflects the individual taste, interest, and decision making of the owner. Take a day and wander around looking at people's gardens. Note the variety of designs and layouts. Admire wildflower color explosions and contrast them with the pristine, orderly, monochromatic pattern of just one flower.

Every day you make countless decisions that reflect the uniquely human spirit of creativity. Can we become more aware of such a precious gift? Can we do things to strengthen that unique quality? You bet we can!

Enjoy these four little hints, four little exercises (aerobics for the mind) to strengthen our creative powers, just for plain *fun*!

The first hint is to train yourself to ask yourself (and your students), "What else?" No matter what you're

doing/thinking/planning, whisper, "What else?" to yourself, and (unless you are in a comatose state) your brain
will begin whirling: What else can we add to this idea?
What else can we combine? What else will connect? What
else can we think of for our party? trip? theme? reunion?
poem? story? program? When you ask "What else?"
you help dissolve the negative, closed-minded, shrinking
smugness of "It's finished!" or "We've already done that!"
or "I can't think of anything else!" *Booo* to that kind of
antonym of creativity! Train yourself to be open, courageous, willing to be playful, experimental, willing to be
surprised. "What else?" kindles the flames of delight and
discovery, such important components of the creative
process.

The second hint is the question, "What if?" I call
these two words the words of *wonder*. What if you turned
your room into a rain forest? into an ocean? into a time
machine? What if you could understand the language
of animals? What if you could communicate with your
ancestors? What if you could be invisible? "What if?" is, as
all great questions are, limitless in its possibilities. "What
if?" is inspiration for the imagination. "What if?" will take
you on marvelous, exciting journeys you may need to record, illustrate, map, sketch, paint, dance, sing, describe,
dramatize. (I could go on . . . and . . . on . . .)

Moving on to our third hint: "Show the idea!" Howard Gardner, in his multiple intelligences theory, helps
strengthen our thinking in this most fascinating area. We
humans have *so many* ways to *show* an idea! We aren't
limited to instinctual patterns. We have language, visual

arts, kinesthetic awareness. We are poets, builders, dancers, architects, construction workers, philosophers. We can express or communicate an idea in countless ways—why be limited to just one or two? Show the idea, using a poster, a chart, a T-shirt, a bumper sticker, a mobile, a book, a construction, a sand sculpture, or a song. Free yourself! Mess around with ideas! Be playful! Be open to the myriad possibilities!

This last little hint may seem frivolous, but trust me, it's truly helpful: "If you think you can't do it, pretend you can." *Fake it! Try it! Just do it!* This is about courage! Don't shrivel your spirit with self-defeating excuses. Risk! Experiment! Be willing to make the effort without fear of criticism or self-doubt or ridicule (enemies of creativity). Surprise yourself! Set a great example for your students. "Hey kids, I'm *not* Walt Whitman or Langston Hughes or Edna St. Vincent Millay, but golly I'm going to have a grand time trying my hand at writing poetry. Join me! I'm going to *pretend* I can write a poem! Wow! Did I write that? (Not bad!)"

Life is short. Fill it with memorable, exciting moments. Encourage your students to live their lives to the fullest, to enjoy the ordinary, everyday, miraculous opportunities life offers us to be the most we can. I tell the kids (borrowing from the United Negro College Fund's wonderful motto), "Our minds, time, and talents are terrible things to waste!" Expand your thinking about that "C" word. It's an integral part of your identity, your *self.*

Surprise yourself. And, if you think you can't, *fake it!*

Hurrying through the halls

to the kindergarten room for my next Artists-in-Schools session, I hear calypso rhythms wafting through the closed door of the classroom I'm looking for. I knock, but no one answers, so I just go in.

"Day-o!" Pulsing steel drums and the bouncy lyrics of the "Banana Boat Song" fill the air as swaying children glide and dance around the room, singing along, twirling and stepping, smiling and improvising. I set down my own records, tambourine, and puppet, and join their dance. When the song is over, we clap and hug. Shining faces greet me. I look around for the teacher and spot her still sitting at her desk, putting away papers. I grin at her.

"Such fun. What's going on?"

"Oh, we're just killing time," she answers.

Old trooper that I am, I plunge right into my hour with the kindergartners. Still soaring and delighted from the joy of the "Banana Boat Song," we continue moving, singing, playing, dancing, and telling stories. But something chips away at the happiness I feel from being with the children. The words *killing time* gnaw at my spirit.

If we could interview each and every child in that class, I'd bet my life that every one of them would say the best part of that day, perhaps the best part of the school year thus far, was our short, precious period spent singing and dancing together. Yet without malice, hurtful intentions, or conscious negativism, their teacher described the activity as "killing time."

In those few minutes of singing and dancing, so much happened and so many skills were called on: total participation and cooperation, freedom of expression, oral language, reviewing information (the lyrics, which everyone already knew), rhythm, small- and gross-motor skills, listening skills, multicultural education, sequential learning, patterning, verbal skills, respecting the space of others, repetition, and—most important—enjoyment.

Think for a moment about your own school experiences. Think about those few minutes before a guest arrives at your classroom door, when you and the children exchange ideas, anticipate, wonder what the person will be like, wonder how the visit will go, suggest questions to ask. Do you consider that to be killing time? Perhaps those moments are the peak times.

Consider the song you sing together in the few minutes before the bell rings for assembly; the anecdotes children share before daily morning exercises officially begin; the complicated hand-clap/rap/chant songs the children teach each other in the few minutes of free time between getting drinks and the math lesson; the drawing, writing, sharing, talking, and joking time after lunch on a rainy day when outside recess is called off. Killing time or peak time?

Here are some "in-between" times recorded in my journal and imprinted on my memory:

- ✳ Pnina standing against the classroom wall, waiting to hang her coat, the sun shining on her back, explaining, "I love my shadow."
- ✳ Len playing the "Hokey Pokey" on his "violin" in those few seconds before the story begins.
- ✳ Ben bringing in the bird's nest his grandpa found—even though it wasn't sharing day.
- ✳ Antonio calling his classmates to the window to see the rarely seen white squirrel, just as quiet time is over and reading groups begin. "It looks like a ghost squirrel," observes Dylan with wide wonder in his eyes.
- ✳ Callie and Chloe sitting at their table during that waiting time before attendance is called, counting the little stones Callie keeps in her jacket pocket.
- ✳ Kindergartners joyful together, dancing and swirling to the "Banana Boat Song" as the Artist-in-School arrives.

Killing time? Peak time? Prime time? Hallowed time? Sometimes those incidental, in-between, hang-loose, unstructured, spontaneous times together are our best times. Perhaps the children (and we) will remember those times longest and with the most fondness.

Right now, on this day-o, what time is it in your classroom? How do you tell your time?

Why I'm Still Hanging Out with the Kids

It always tickles me when folks I meet ask, "Are you still hanging out with little kids?" as if there's some cosmic cutoff time to get on with one's life and commit to more in-depth professions! I've long past that cutout date. My claim to fame is longevity and postponement of closure! I usually respond something like this: "Am I still hanging out with little kids? Is the sky still up? Is water still wet? Of course, darling, till my last breath!"

This question challenges me to examine my reasons for doing what I do, to clarify and explain my beliefs, to help me touch base.

I don't know about you, but one of the main reasons I hang around little kids is that I never know or can predict what they'll say or do. They haven't yet received their scripts for life, for their roles in the great drama! They're just beginning to learn the ways, the whys, the whats on their minds. (Why do we say *on* our minds instead of *in* our minds? Oh, well . . .)

Being with little kids is an antidote to smugness. You've got to be on your toes when they're around. You can't be cool! Polite conversation is a benchmark goal. Poetic, creative use of language is their gift. They are just beginning to dip their toes into the sea of conformity. They're still originals! Little kids tell you things like "My birthday is coming to my house next week!" (Cheyenne) They ask questions like "Daddy, do you remember when you first saw me?" (Noah) They respond to instructions to pick up their rooms with, "Mommy I'm not the person for this!" (Domenico) They pay a mourning call on a grieving neighbor by consoling him with "Is your dog still dead?" (Tonya)

They comfort you with existential challenges. Some years ago, my then ninety-five-year-old mother and I were grabbing lunch at a fast-food restaurant. Nearby, two kids and their moms were doing the same. We ate and waved and smiled at the two three-year-olds, who waved and smiled back at us. One of the two, Jamie, hung over the booth, peering into our eyes, and finally asked, "Are you old or new?"

Mom and I hastily bit into our sandwiches to avoid giving an immediate answer. These are the questions you imagine puzzling over in an advanced philosophy course you might take in graduate school. These are the questions of heavy-duty essay assignments that forbid one-syllable responses. Chewing slowly, I munched over some

possible answers for the waiting Grand Inquisitor, still
devoting his total concentration to us!

Here are some unacceptable possible answers that
would earn you an incomplete in that imaginary philosophy course:

> Old in years, but New in possibilities.
> Old in experiences, but New in whatever is in store.
> Old in yesterdays, but New in todays and tomorrows.
> Old in feelings, but New in dreams.
> Old in fears, but New in hopes.
> Old in memories, but New in beginnings.
> Old in habits, but New in breaking habits.
> Old in the known, but New in the unknown.
> Old in old tricks, but New in adventures.
> Old in learning, but New in unlearning.
> Old in being, but New in becoming.
> Old in hibernating, but New in emerging.
> Old in what I forgot, but New in what I remember.

"What do you think, Jamie? Are we old or new?"

The adorable little guy bit into his chicken nugget.
We knew he was contemplating the many ways he could
answer *our* challenge. Thankfully, before he was able to
share his wisdom, his insight, his perception, his revela-
tion, thankfully, his mom called him to finish his fries.
Whew! A close call!

Those of us who like to hang out with little kids teeter-
totter on the edge. We live dangerously.

Walking to the car with my mother, I thought of all
the "old" teachers with years of experience in their hearts,

minds, and hands. Their energy, openness, and willingness to risk and to try unfamiliar, new ideas are boundless.
Their stubborn commitment to their beliefs and their
promises to teach in joyful and loving ways in the midst of
devastating pressures to avoid the scenic route and keep to
the narrow limits of test-driven schedules and curriculum
are inspiring. Yes, they may be "old" in years, but they
are very, very new in spirit. I am sadly reminded of a few
very new young teachers already rigid in their methods
and goals, narrow in their views of children, unwilling to
share and exchange materials and ideas.

They may be "new" in years, but they are old, old, old.

We turned and waved good-bye again to the children.
Jamie grinned at us through the window and showed
us his cookie. We were relieved that sometimes young
children have short attention spans. We hoped that when
we next met up with that little group, Jamie would *not*
remember his ear-shattering, mind-boggling, bare-bones
question: "Are you old or new?"

(And what are you?)

Despite such traumatic encounters with the spontaneous, unpredictable, totally honest, pure curiosity of our
lunchtime pals, I still hang out with little kids!

(Do you?)

Acknowledgments

My claim to fame is longevity and fear of closure! Let's
add fear of brevity! I could fill thick catalogs with names
of colleagues, friends, neighbors, family, and children who
helped me on this road we're all walking together, who
kept the flames of hope and joy burning! If time and space
permitted, I could easily thank everyone I have ever met
in my whole life!

And some I haven't met! So let me start by thank-
ing our human ancestors, those amazing cave dwellers
who somehow mysteriously and miraculously found ways
to paint pictures, make music, tell stories, choreograph
dances, and shape objects in dark, prehistoric times! They
taught us the oldest, most natural and basic ways our
human family learns, teaches, celebrates, and communi-
cates. We're still in our cave waiting for fire to be found,
but we're keeping warm by dancing, singing, storytelling,
and making art together!

Keeping that sacred tradition alive are many programs that honor our children and the healthy, arts-rich
ways they best learn. I'm so glad these programs have *not*
counted our years together but just keep on renewing the
involvement of this old hippie!

Thank you, Leo Yassenoff Jewish Community Center,
Columbus, Ohio. Carol Folkerth, executive director, Tim

Kauffman, associate director, and Barbara Topolosky, director, assisted by Taryn Twillger, Nikki Henry, and the fabulous staff in our NAEYC-accredited early childhood program, have made possible many moving moments. Special thanks to our administrative assistant, Sherie Mescher, who organized the trio of adorable children on the cover of this book: Trenton Hunter, Nora Butter, and Eli Helfgott. Thanks, Allen Zak, for delighting the children with your laughter-inspiring aerobics to catch the wonderful photo.

I honor the late Ray Hanley, who directed the Greater Columbus Arts Council with fierce dedication, courage, and spirit. Thanks also to Tim Katz, Terry Anderson, Jim Arter, and Oulanje Regan, who coordinate the GCAC's Artists-in-Schools and Children of the Future programs, for letting me be a part of all the joyful times all these years. Their vision for our children and the vital importance of the arts in their lives and in the life of our community has never wavered.

Almost thirty years ago, Phil Boiarski, Aaron Leventhal, Larry Hamill, and I planted a tiny seed we called Days of Creation (DOC)—Arts for Kids. That seed has bloomed and blossomed. Through DOC camps, festivals, and school programs, thousands of kids have fallen in love with the arts, inspired by our roster of outstanding artists/educators under the leadership of Kaye Boiarski. Thank you, all, for my glorious years with Days!

And thank you to the Education Department of Otterbein College for continuous opportunities to share my summer course, Arts Across the Curriculum. Niki Fayne, former chairperson of the department, started that summer adventure years ago. Malene Deringer, chairperson, with a big help from Claire Parson and Katherine Reichley and their staff, put up with all the crazy creativity every summer. Thanks for your patience and cheerful indulgence! To all the students over all the years—keep the spirit! Hugs!

Another program so dear to my heart and inspiring to children, teachers, and community is DepARTures, a unique collaboration between the Columbus Public Schools and the Columbus Museum of Art, launched almost twenty years ago by Carole Genshaft, former director of education for the museum. Museum director Nannette Maciejunes and Columbus public schools superintendent Gene Harris are to be commended for supporting DepARTures over these many years. I'm grateful to Barbara Sweney, Cindy Foley, Jessimi Jones, and their fabulous colleagues from the museum—docents, guards, and volunteers—as well as to teachers and administrators in the Columbus schools, for all the work and love and for letting me be one of the DepARTure poets. With my fellow poets Terry Hermsen, Dionne Custer, Nancy Kangas, and Nancy Minter, thousands of our fifth graders have discovered the power and beauty of the arts. I've learned so much from our DepARTure students and from all of you.

WOSU, Columbus's National Public Radio affiliate, has opened its studios to me over many years. Special thanks to Fred Andrle, who hosts WOSU's *Open Line,* for welcoming my passionate opinions about children and education and for giving me the opportunity to be an advocate for everything I believe.

Polly Greenberg, former editor of *Young Children* and a trailblazing educator and author, gave me pages in that outstanding journal for my rants and raves. She is and has been one of my heroes in her consistent, powerful advocacy for our children. Thank you, Derry Koralek, editor of *Young Children,* for continuing to make room for my literary outbursts. We need all the voices raised for our kids!

Outstanding role models and pillars of inspiration like Bertha Campbell, Ella Jenkins, Alice Sterling Honig, Mary Rivkin, and Mary Renck Jalongo continue to lead and guide. We need their wisdom!

O my! My hand trembles. You superlative teachers of all grades and ages! My joy is to celebrate your "works" with children of all ages and in all grades. Please forgive me in advance, as I know I can't name you all; limited name-dropping will have to suffice: Marlene Robbins (my Marween), Maureen Reedy, Tom Griffin, Cathy Arment, Ronni Spratt, Rose Stough, Tom Tenerovich, Janis Pechenik, Lorraine Arcus, and Dawn Heyman must represent you in this note of love and appreciation.

All of our nationally known music makers are to be honored! They infuse the lives of us all with such joy. I want to thank our "neighborhood" troubadours for their gifts to our children: Leslie Zak, Joan Calen, Mark Wilder, Marc Rossio, Debbie (rainbow girl) Clement. Keep singing! We need you! Thanks, music maker Enrique Feldman, for spreading the message of music and the arts to neighborhoods across the country.

Thank you to Angie May Brewer, Lea Ann Hall, and the wonderful friends giving time, talent, and energy to the Columbus Association for the Education of Young Children. Kim Tice, Amy Eldridge, and the Ohio Association for the Education of Young Children—thanks for putting up with my cave technology!

To Cicily Sweet, Adit Granite, and my fabulous folk dancers in OSU Hillel's international folk dance program, thanks for keeping the dancing going when I had to go on the road! And thanks for always welcoming children of all ages into our dancing circles.

To dear friends, neighbors, and community members who always care and are ready to support our causes—thanks! Our kids need us!

To my sister, Laura Walcher, a loving (but mean!) editor; to my sister-in-love, Marilyn Cohen (the chick lady), a master teacher; to my brother, Mike Kaplan, who always laughs at my jokes; to Bob Walcher and Herb Cohen, my brothers-in-law, who are in the brotherhood; to my poster child for creativity, Michael Joel Rosen; to my niece, Caryn Falvey, an enlightened and loving principal; to the family tribes Chenfelds, Cohens, Kaplans, Blooms, Walchers, O'Briens, Wilbats, Rappoports, Falveys, Gandals, Newmans, Selingers, Jacobsons—I love you!

To each and all of you who have walked and talked with me along the way throughout the country and world, sharing your stories, wisdom, and hopes. I am humbled by that honor.

Sid Farrar, editor-in-chief at Redleaf Press, and Carol Copple, director of publications for NAEYC, have been wonderful, professional, and supportive friends of this book, of children, of teachers, and of me. You and the wonderful editorial staff at Redleaf Press (Jeni Henrickson, Laurie Herrmann, Emily Nesheim, and especially Ryan Huber Scheife for his design magic) and at NAEYC have made this new book possible! Keep celebrating!

First, last, and always, Howard.

Credit Lines

Born in New York City in 1935, Mimi has devoted most of her life to being with friends of all ages, backgrounds, and abilities, in every kind of setting, from playgrounds to prisons, from Head Start to Upward Bound, from infant and toddler programs to senior centers, from New York to Hawaii. She has shared her message of loving, joyful learning and celebration in almost fifty states and several countries.

In 1970 she moved to Columbus, Ohio, with her husband, Howard, and their three children, Cara, Dan, and Cliff. She continues to be deeply involved in the cultural and educational life of central Ohio.

Mimi's nonfiction books, *Creative Experiences for Young Children* (Heinemann, 2002), *Teaching by Heart* (Redleaf Press, 2001), and *Teaching in the Key of Life* (NAEYC, 1993), are widely used. Her children's novel, *The House at 12 Rose Street* (Abelard-Schuman, 1966), adapted for television and nominated for an Emmy, was one of the first stories for children dealing with race relations, civil rights, and peer pressure.

She is the humble recipient of numerous awards, but the honor still closest to her heart came from a child who said, "Mimi, you're the queen of fun!"